The Big Book Of

GIN

Dan Jones

hardie grant books

Welcome To The Big Book Of Gin   7

A Flash Of Lightning: The Curious Story Of Gin   9

How It's Made   12

1 THE WORLD'S BEST GINS, TONICS & MIXERS 116

The World's Best Gins   18

The World's Best Tonics & Mixers   34

2 THE TOOL BOX   40

The Essentials   42

The Luxuries   44

A Guide To Glasses   46

How To Do It: Cocktail Tricks   50

3 INFUSIONS, SYRUPS, SOURS & BRINES   52

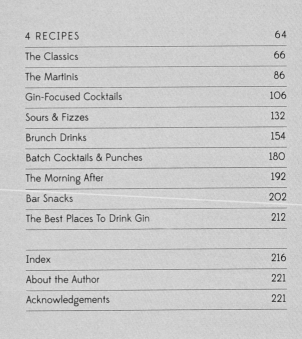

4 RECIPES	64
The Classics	66
The Martinis	86
Gin-Focused Cocktails	106
Sours & Fizzes	132
Brunch Drinks	154
Batch Cocktails & Punches	180
The Morning After	192
Bar Snacks	202
The Best Places To Drink Gin	212
Index	216
About the Author	221
Acknowledgements	221

WELCOME
TO THE
BIG BOOK
OF GIN

This is *The Big Book of Gin*. How to mix it, shake it, stir it and – most importantly – how to drink it.

From its troubled birth on the slimy backstreets of ye olde London to its current incarnation as the world's fastest-growing artisanal spirit, gin's salacious past and rosy future are as thirst-quenching as a freshly made G & T.

Today, there are hundreds of producers, from old-school mega-brands headed up by legendary master distillers to small-batch makers, backyard boilers and kitchen tinkerers. And with indie tonics, powerful syrups and exotic sodas, there's never been so many ways to drink gin. Gin can be fiery with a lip-curling bitterness, cloyingly floral as nanna's knicker drawer, or as verdantly herbal as an attic weed farm, but the crystal-clear spirit is best when it relies on its subtleties. The best producers, no matter their size or how passionate their approach, are those that achieve a heavenly balance of essential, traditional ingredients with their own contemporary collection of botanicals.

The *Big Book of Gin* celebrates this magical spirit with a full list of enthusiastic amateur mix-at-home recipes (see page 64), infusions and syrups (see page 51), with essential and impressive tools (see page 42), glassware (see page 46), marvellous mixers (see page 34), butt-tingling bitters, delicious bar snacks and small plates (see page 202), and the world's very best gins (see page 18), from English, Scottish and Spanish classics to international megabrands and fresh, young indie upstarts from the UK to Australia and the States.

Now, let's drink gin.

A FLASH

OF LIGHTNING:

THE CURIOUS

STORY OF GIN

Gin has a steamy, love/hate relationship with London, the greatest city on Earth (indisputable, if you've had a few). Not so long ago, gin was the English capital's fun-juice of choice, and yet it had a rather dour reputation. Instead of its refined contemporary incarnation, in Georgian England it was suckled by cackling, wooden-toothed wastrels, pox-ridden poets and general London lowlifes. For those attracted to the bright lights of the big city, the streets weren't paved with gold but listless bodies of drunks (captured to satirical effect in Hogarth's infamous 1751 prints *Beer Street* and *Gin Lane*). But how did the delicious spirit become such a popular tipple? And why London?

The story begins in the low countries. Gin's distant ancestor is the lively Dutch tipple known as Genever, much loved across Holland, Belgium and northern France in the 1500s. But in 1572 the dashing Professor Sylvius de Bouve created his own neutral-distilled spirit with notes of juniper and malt wine, now known as Genever. It remains the traditional drink of the Netherlands, the sailors' fiery sip of 'Dutch courage', and is the inspiration behind modern gin.

Back in London, the favoured pick-me-up was a nip of delicious French brandy, but in the late 1600s the UK's King William III, aka the be-wigged Dutchman William of Orange, changed all that. His beef with the French saw him ban the import of the nation's brandies into the UK. To make up for the unpopular dearth of tasty booze, William gave his British subjects a gift: he did away with licensing laws, allowing the magic of the distillation process to be available to all, from professional booze-makers to home enthusiasts. This relaxation of the rules created a generation of moonshine-makers and soon Londoners did what they do best: got horribly, impossibly drunk. The poor and down-on-their-luck were tantalised by Genever, popular with the upper classes. With the real thing out of their reach, they sought to make their own and soon their dry, clear concoction became as available as drinking water, if not more so.

With a bit of basic distillation kit, low-quality gin could be made in your own home, and was sold across London in grimy taverns, squalid drinking rooms, barbershops, brothels and Mother Clap's infamous Molly House, the city's sauciest drinking venue. Gin gave Londoners a twinkle in their eye, a spring in their step, and wrested the city into a binge-drinking crisis.

By the early-to-mid-1700s, the 'Gin Craze' was in its stride and an eye-popping 45.5 million litres (10 million gallons) of gin was distilled annually in the capital, with each crossed-eyed Londoner drinking around 63.5 million litres (14 gallons) each year. London's death rate overtook its birth rate, as poverty and the gullet-melting cheap gin sold in the taverns and backstreets of the capital's seediest neighbourhoods took hold.

Sensing a gin-powered armageddon, the government was forced to draw up society-saving legislation. The Gin Act of 1751 came into force, controls were added, and an outright ban on distillation for a couple of years saw the price of gin shoot up.

Public health may have improved but nothing could dent Londoners' love of gin. In the early 1800s, Aeneas Coffey invented the column still, and gin got a tasty upgrade. The new, improved spirit became the centrepiece of a new wave of sparkling gin palaces: slick drinking dens, bright and gas-lit with ornate façades, shining out in the gloom of the streets. Inside, Londoners could escape the drudgery of city life, knocking back a tipple – known as a 'quick flash of lightning' – cheaper than they could beer.

Gin and flavoured mixers evolved into classy long drinks and clever cocktails. Colonial Brits returning from new worlds introduced exotic ingredients (bitter anti-malarial quinine was mixed with gin and sugar in a precursor to the gin and tonic) and the Gimlet, a cocktail of gin and lime juice, was said to ward off scurvy. Gin's reputation was on the up. By the mid-1800s, the exclusive Garrick Club had mastered a gin punch, and cocktail parties replaced the boring formality of Edwardian dinner parties. Forward to the 1930s and 'Bright Young Things' like Stephen Tennant were drinking gin cocktails (in between snifters of 'naughty salt', no doubt).

The young Queen Mother's famous love of gin had also marked out the spirit with an unofficial royal concoction. Yet, by the 60s, gin had a bit of a PR problem. Despite its rough-edged beginnings, it had become associated with the upper classes and had acquired uncomfortable colonial connotations. Quality nose-dived, too, and gin seemed to flatline.

In recent years, craft-edged enterprising indie brands have reanimated the spirit's fortunes, bringing back gin's history of under-the-counter experimentations with modern equipment and fragrant organic botanicals. The UK – the world's leading gin-producing nation – now exports an impressively huge quantity of the spirit to new markets that have become obsessed with artisanal versions of the spirit and thoughtfully made mixers. British gin – along with excellent US and European brands – is having a bit of a moment and in the most surprising places: Spaniards are obsessed, Colombians are crazy for it. London's most famous export (after the Spice Girls, obviously) has come a long way from the backstreets of its most squalid neighbourhoods, but it's never lost its spark: that flash of lightning.

HOW IT'S MADE

Although gin-makers tend to keep their exact recipe a closely guarded secret, they're usually rather proud of their ingredients, powered by a clever combination of botanicals. This can include anything from coriander (cilantro), Angelica and orange peel to lemon peel, cardamom, cinnamon, cubeb pepper and nutmeg – with juniper berries as a must-have. Modern makers tweak this recipe and – with their own distillation processes, timings, vintage equipment and purified water – their own subtly distinct gin is born.

London Gin, aka London Dry Gin, is what most of us mix in our G & Ts. Although the spirit isn't a product of origin (i.e. it can be made anywhere in the world), the name is legally defined – it must be 80 proof, or 37.5 per cent ABV (alcohol by volume), with absolutely no unnatural ingredients and, post-distillation, no added flavourings or colourings. Just a tiny amount of sugar is permitted, making it very dry.

Gin distillation has two main processes: column-distilled and pot-stilled. Perhaps the most popular are pot-still gins – the sexy, curvaceous copper pots are given female nicknames – like Angela and Wilma – with vintage ones held in high regard. The copper is important: the metal reacts with alcohol and helps get rid of any impurities, removing the need to filter at the end so that all the flavour and character is retained. Distilled gin is different in that makers add flavourings after distillation, often in infusion bags, to give a soft, mellow taste (this means some backyard makers can purchase a plain spirit and mix at home).

They begin with a strong base spirit – alcohol that began as a grain, like barley, maize or even molasses – then water is used to dilute (some producers use rarified water for this step, from secret local springs, even glaciers), and botanicals are added. The distillation process involves slowly heating the liquid until the alcohol evaporates and winds its way through a still before condensing – allowing it to be captured and separating it from the water. The addition of botanicals (whole, in clever little infusion bags, or on a tray above the liquid) means the vaporised spirit becomes infused with pungent flavours, curious aromas and unique character. Imagine a steamy, lusty 1970s San Franciscan sauna and you're halfway there.

Increasingly, craft gin-makers are using the still-rare 'one-shot' distillation method, a geeky, fastidious approach that gives pinpoint control over the final product. One-shotters infuse their base spirit with botanicals and let the mixture macerate for hours – often overnight. Once the flavours have steeped into the spirit and it has taken on a murky, oily quality, it's ready for distilling. Makers often like to use the 'heart' or middle run of the process, discarding the alcohol collected at the beginning and end of distillation to create the smoothest, purest drop possible.

1

The World's

Best Gins, Mixers & Tonics

THE WORLD'S BEST
GINS

From age-old classics and steadfast sippers to
bright, innovative upstarts and the small batch
indie brands that are a real labour of love.

58 Gin

Gin-lover turned gin-maker Mark Marmont opts for single-shot distillation for his legendary, award-winning 58 Gin – where the 'head' and 'tail' of the gin are discarded (the spirit created at the beginning and end of the process) leaving only the 'heart'. Hand-labelled and wonkily wax sealed, with artwork by larger-than-life London tattoo artist Mo Coppoletta, 58 uses nine pungent botanicals including juniper, coriander (cilantro), lemon, pink grapefruit, vanilla, orris root, cubeb pepper, bergamot and Angelica. The result is a verdant, fresh spirit with a little citrus, pepper and pine nuts, a touch of sweetness and a big meaty slap of juniper at the end.

Four Pillars

Three gin-loving mates decided to give it a good Aussie go and make their own – and their crowdfunded Four Pillars Gin is a little ripper. Created in a pot-still named Wilma, using triple-filtered water from the Yarra Valley, Australia, and a curious recipe of botanicals, it is local, exotic and traditional. Cinnamon, cardamom and juicy whole oranges power this delicious gin with its fresh juniper hit and Tasmanian pepper berry, lemon myrtle, star anise and floral lavender, yet after distillation, it rests in French oak barrels for three to six months. Wilma is a CARL still: he tip-top, very best still in the business, so Four Pillars is a supremely smooth and bright drop.

Martin Miller's

Meet Angela, gin-maker Martin Miller's curvy vintage pot-still used to make his super-fresh spirit via a unique recipe of botanicals and a geeky dual process (where the earthier botanical ingredients are distilled separately from the lighter, citrus notes). Angela ensure's Miller's gin has an incredible depth of flavour with each element able to shine through. He adds Tuscan juniper, cassia bark, Angelica, Florentine orris, coriander (cilantro), Seville citrus peel, nutmeg, cinnamon and liquorice root to the mix with pure Icelandic spring water. Thanks, Angela!

Moonshine Kid's Dogs Nose

Cold-distilled under vacuum, with Chinook and Columbus hops and an edit of classic botanicals, Moonshine Kid's Dogs Nose Gin has coriander (cilantro), lemon, juniper and borage to lend a hoppy, creamy feel, plus a little spice for good measure. Creator Matt Whiley, aka the Moonshine Kid, is a founding member of Fluid Movement, the creatives behind a range of contemporary cocktail bars, and his Dogs Nose Gin is made right at the very heart of the spirit's London birthplace. It's a real mixer's drop and is delicious in cocktails.

NO. 209

No. 209 is many things: the 209th distillery to be registered in the United States, one of the world's finest small-batch, handcrafted spirit-makers and, perhaps, the only Kosher-for-Passover gin creator in the world. Distilled four times, No. 209's citrus and spice taste comes from bergamot, lemon peel, cardamom pods, cassia bark, Angelica root and coriander seeds, along with a powerful punch of juniper. Winemakers by trade, 209 also age gin in used wine barrels, and their No. 209 Cabernet Sauvignon Barrel Reserve Gin has a magical amber hue. *Mazel tov!*

Butler's Lemongrass & Cardamom

Inspired by ye olde Victorian recipe, Butler's is an infused gin that uses a 20-litre (5¼-gallon) infusion jar and a truck-load of fresh lemongrass, cardamom, coriander (cilantro), cloves, cinnamon, star anise, fennel, lemon and lime – tied up in infusion bags. Based in Hackney Wick, the East London industrial neighbourhood whose grimy countenance is in sharp contrast to its shiny neighbour, the Olympic Park, the Butler's team hand bottle their strongly perfumed (yet delicately flavoured) spirit after 18 hours. It's a place for outcasts and oddballs and the perfect base for Butler's Gin, an artisan spirit with a little East End swagger. Butler's has a pale yellow-green tone and is best served chilled, with cucumber. A refined concoction from the wrong side of the tracks.

Conker Spirit

Like it smooth? Rupert Holloway sure does. The one-time chartered surveyor (aka brick counter) opened the first gin distillery in Dorset, UK, and has set about making 60-bottle batches of what is perhaps the UK's smoothest, softest, and most off-beat gin, the Dorset Dry. A British wheat spirit with a classic juniper base, Rupert uses hand-picked local gorse flowers (instead of liquorice or cardamom) for a soft vanilla edge, elderberries and samphire that, when distilled, has a subtle salted caramel taste. Conker also produce a cold-brew coffee liqueur sweetened with a touch of demerara, but it's the smoother-than-smooth award-winning Dorset Dry you'll fall for.

Bathtub Gin

In the sad, dry days of North American prohibition, gin-lovers would make illicit concoctions in their bathtubs – harsh enough to strip the enamel – and drink them until their eyes glazed over. Inspired by this dedicated yet obsessive method, US-made Bathtub Gin is created in tiny batches using a copper pot-still and is packed with juniper and orange, coriander (cilantro), cardamom, cloves and cinnamon. This is a strong and confident drop with subtle, well-balanced flavours and a soft, creamy feel, which is leagues away from its bathtub beginnings. Winner of the World's Best Compound Gin at the 2015 World Gin Awards, booze brand Professor Cornelius Ampleforth should feel rather proud.

Salcombe Gin Start Point

Crafted by two childhood sailing buddies in the coastal town of Salcombe, South Devon (think the Hamptons of the UK), this delicious premium brand has its own impressive distillery, gin school and bar, and uses pure, soft spring water from the wilds of Dartmoor National Park. The gin itself is a London Dry via an interesting clash of classic botanicals with a power-punch of Macedonian juniper and exotic citrus including ruby grapefruit, lemon and lime – a nod to Salcombe's fruit traders of yore. In fact, ruby grapefruit is Salcombe's recommended citrus twist for a Start Point martini. Smooth and complex with a premium taste.

Monkey 47

It takes a tough little monkey to knock back this modern legend from the Black Forest. This award-winning, toe-curling, eye-popping and mouth-caving gin is 47 proof and has a complex, woody flavour with a fruity, spicy, peppery and herby finish and a cranberry kick for good measure. Taking inspiration from classical British gin, Indian influences, the fairytale woods of the Black Forest and, um, monkeys, there are 47 ingredients to enjoy. It may sound rather complex, but this monkey is perfectly balanced, using locally sourced spring water for a fresh touch.

Collagin

Remember the magical elixir from 90s comic-horror movie, *Death Becomes Her* that granted everlasting life to two age-allergic glamazons? This is the contemporary version. Collagin from the UK's Young in Spirit (founded by 'gintrepreneurs' and gal pals Camilla Brown and Liz Beswick) is the world's first collagen-combined spirit. Eleven delicate botanicals infuse warm, earthy liquorice and notes of orris and vanilla, balanced with juniper and fresh, juicy orange, and a hefty amount of (flavourless) marine collagen. Whether Collagin will give you the power of everlasting beauty is unclear, but it makes a delicious, velvety G & T.

Beefeater 24

That most British (by way of China and India) of drinks: the cup of tea is the inspiration behind Beefeater 24. Created in the heart of London, the well-known gin brand took 18 months to perfect a recipe that includes Japanese sencha tea and Chinese green tea. Its complex botanicals – from Seville orange peel, grapefruit and lemon peel to juniper, coriander seed, liquorice, Angelica root, almond and orris root – are steeped for a full 24 hours, hence the name. Aromatic in the extreme with a smooth finish.

Goldy

To Australia, where Sydney restaurateur and hotelier Maurice Terzini and inked-up fashion influencer Justin O'Shea have created Goldy Gin, a confident newcomer that has a surprisingly smooth and classic taste with little of the jiggery-pokery you might expect from such an Insta-famous duo. The recipe for Goldy was developed with Tony Conigliaro, the force behind London bars 69 Colebrooke Row and Bar Termini, and the gin itself is straight-to-the-point, powerful and tasty. Woody with bright citrus and a smooth finish.

Hayman's 1850 Reserve

Hayman's Reserve harks back to the debauched gin palaces of old, channelling the flavour and aroma of the spirit as it was in 1850. Lucky, then, that the Hayman family have been in the British gin business since 1863. Christopher Hayman's small brand is powered by a deep love of the spirit, a catalogue of secret recipes, and Chris's son James and daughter Miranda. Subtle and smooth, Hayman's classic gin recipe is aged in wood for a soft, mellow flavour with notes of juniper and coriander (cilantro), a little black pepper and a subtle touch of spice.

Gin Mare

Using rosemary, thyme, basil and a truck-load of olives, Gin Mare has infused the true spirit of the Mediterranean into the Gin & Tonic. This is a Spanish gin created in Vilanova, a small fishing village in Spain (soon to be one of the biggest gin markets in the world). Crafted by the Ribot family who have been making spirits since the late 1800s (their Gin MG, launched in the 1940s, is one of Spain's top-selling spirits), Gin Mare is intended to push the classic London Dry recipe to its outer limits. With family-grown juniper berries, Gin Mare is a clever, herbal spirit that's become a huge hit in Spain and the rest of the gin-drinking world.

Bloom

Master Distiller Joanne Moore (one of the few known female master distillers in the world) was inspired by the aroma of English country gardens and wildflower meadows. She created a drop that is insanely floral – packed with honeysuckle, Chinese pomelo (a subtly sweet grapefruit-like citrus fruit) and French chamomile. What's more, Bloom is easy on the juniper, lending it a fresher, less woody taste than trad London Dry Gin. Moore's Bloom is a bit of a show-off on the award circuit – it has scooped up more than 15 gongs, including the prestigious Platinum Medal at the World Spirits Competition in 2010.

The Melbourne Gin Company

Founded in 2012, the Melbourne Gin Company was one of the first Australian gin producers, with founder and former winemaker Andrew Marks playing around with flavours and processes before investing in a delightful copper still from Portugal. Distilling each set of botanicals separately allows for fastidious control; you can create tiny batches of gin to blend into a final product. But who cares when it tastes this good? Along with gin's essential juniper, orris and cassia bark, sniff out honey lemon myrtle, fresh orange, macadamia and a confident hit of rosemary with a little fresh rainwater. Delicious.

Few American Gin

Unlike most gins, Few begins life as a white whiskey – an aged bourbon – and this gives it a completely unique character. With a lemon zest and juniper aroma, Few gives way to a sweet vanilla finish with a clean, pure freshness. This American spirit from the Few craft distillery in Evanston, Illinois (the birthplace of Prohibition), cheekily takes its name from the initials of Frances Elizabeth Willard, a key figure in the Temperance Movement. Few Spirits was the first distillery within the city limits since Prohibition, and the company's diligent approach to creating alcohol is like a popped cork – this distillery is all about creativity and humour. Case in point: their 2015 limited edition Breakfast Gin powered with Earl Grey.

Jinzu

Those that say never mix your drinks have never had Jinzu, the sake/gin hybrid created by young British bartender Dee Davis for drinks mega-brand Diageo's Show Your Spirit competition (it won!). Japanese-inspired botanicals, from cherry blossom to yuzu, dominate and Dee's artful blend with Junmai sake lends the spirit a deliciously creamy flavour. Initially distilled under Tanqueray's Master Distiller in Scotland, Jinzu is inspired, in part, by Dee's first trip to Japan when she was just 16. Bright citrus, cherry blossom florals, and a soft juniper for classicists.

Bath Gin

Created by the Canary Gin Bar in Bath, England – in small-batch numbered bottles – this delightful gin's use of wormwood and kaffir lime leaf is inspired, creating a considered, premium gin that is worthy of Jane Austen herself. With Jane winking out from its label, Bath Gin is keen to underline its literary pretensions and affiliation with Bath, the English UNESCO World Heritage city, but it's the tasty botanicals that excite: cassia bark, lemon peel, smoky burnt orange peel, cubeb berry, liquorice, cardamom, angelica root and juniper. Austen, no doubt, would have loved a little pick-me-up between chapters.

Hendrick's

Hendrick's is the extremely small batch, pot-still distilled and blended Scottish juniper gin with an intimate relationship with cucumber. Small-batch gin is usually made approximately 1,000 litres (220 gallons) at a time; Hendrick's plump for just half that, using two vintage stills, which means the brand's gin-tasters have greater control over the flavour of each pot. Heavy on the cucumber, Hendrick's has discovered the aromatic vegetable's perfect flavourmate: the rose (or Bulgarian *Rosa Damascena*, to be exact). Usually served steeped with macerated cucumber and even more delicious for it.

The One Gin

Aromatic sage is the star ingredient in this British dry gin by ethical bottled water company, One, and created by award-winning Master Distiller Sarah Thompson at Blackdown Distillery in Sussex, UK. Funding water projects for more than a decade, The One Foundation aims to raise £20 million by 2020 from One Gin, helping the world's poorest communities gain access to clean drinking water. Lucky, then, that with nine botanicals and seven filtrations, One is incredibly smooth and flavoursome. Let's get tipsy, ethically.

New York Distilling Company Dorothy Parker

Since 2011, New York Distilling Company has created a gin worthy of the lauded writer Dorothy Parker's razor-sharp wit. Dreaming up a drink that would have been the perfect drop to share with Parker, the NYDC blend traditional and contemporary botanicals from a bright, strong juniper and elderberries for the traditionalists, to a surprising hit of hibiscus. Distilled at NYDC's HQ in Brooklyn, a soft, almost spiced cranberry-like edge makes this fruity little number as darkly complex as Parker herself.

Tanqueray No. Ten

There's a reason why Tanqueray, the gin megabrand, seems to be drunk in almost every bar, hotel, and from every airline trolley in the world: it's hands-down delicious. The impressive spirit-maker can produce in eye-watering quantities, but its still finds time to create premium small-batch gin, distilled in its legendary pot, No. 10. Using vintage equipment isn't essential towards creating a delicious gin, but it goes a long way in preserving the art of artisanal gin-making, and the age-old pot distillation process means only small quantities are produced. Tanqueray No. Ten is a classic London Dry Gin, incredibly fragrant and floral and packed with zingy citrus. Nice work, Tanqueray.

East London Liquor Company London Dry

Full marks go to founder Alex Wolpert for finding the most Londony London venue to set up his London Dry distillery. In 2013, his East London Liquor Company set up shop in an old glue factory in Bow, East London (look out for the tasteful dead horse reference on the bottle) and began experimenting with recipes, finally producing its first bottled ELLC gin a year later, overseen by head distiller Tom Hills. With two delicious premium versions, even ELLC's core London Dry Gin is gloriously smooth with lemon and grapefruit peel and a little coriander spice.

Highwayman Gin

The house spirit of Ladies & Gentlemen, the tiny cocktail bar in a renovated public toilet in darkest Kentish Town, London, Highwayman Gin is the creation of Vestal Vodka creator William Borrell. Made in a tiny 16-litre (4 gallon) copper still using locally sourced juniper, coriander (cilantro) and Angelica root, the Highwayman is named after Claude Du Val, the 'gentleman thief' who charmed the wallets (and knickers) off rich travellers on the streets of London in the early 17th century. The drop itself is rich and smooth and hands-down the most exciting thing that will ever happen to you in a Kentish Town public toilet.

Caorunn

Scotland in a glass (hold the haggis). Perfectly balanced notes of rowan berry, heather, apple and dandelion make Caorunn (pronounced ka-roon) a unique herbal experience and subtle enough either to sip over ice or enjoy long with a chilled, pared-down and simple tonic, like Schweppes. Lively, fruity flavours and a dry, crisp quality make this small-batch gin utterly delicious. It's conceived in deepest, darkest Scotland at the Balmenach Distillery in Speyside and presented in a chunky, pleasingly weighty bottle that looks mighty fine in anyone's home bar. All in all, a tidy wee drop.

St. George Terroir Gin

Critics' favourite St. George is arguably California's finest spirits producer and their Terroir Gin, created on Mount Tam, is inspired by the Golden State's forested hills and bear-studded nature reserves. Think Douglas fir, bay laurel, coastal sage and roasted coriander seeds; in fact, take a big sip, close your eyes, and you'll be teleported to the misty Californian forests. Could this be the USA's finest premium gin? Does a bear sip in the woods?

Williams Chase

As a young man, Will Chase discovered he had a head for business and a bod for creating the world's best chips. Growing up on a farm in England, amongst fresh, fragrant barley, cider fruit and earthy planting potatoes, Will's crisp brand, Tyrrells (named after the family farm), became world famous. But it's his award-winning gin that's the real stunner. In making Williams Chase gin, Will swapped his much-loved rare potatoes for apples, distilling his own biodynamic apple cider into vodka, and then redistilling it into gin (a lengthy process, but one that produces a unique, fragrant and fresh spirit). There are notes of spice and citrus, cinnamon and nutmeg with a traditional juniper aroma. So, we can thank Will for bringing two magical things into the world: crisps and gin. The man deserves a medal.

The Botanist Islay Dry Gin

The Botanist has, count 'em, 31 botanicals, perfectly balanced to create a delightful little sipper and brilliant mixer. Hailing from the world-famous Bruichladdich distillery on the Scottish Isle of Islay, the Botanist creators match nine traditional botanics with 22 locally sourced, foraged flavours from apple mint to thistle flowers and white clover. Added to a low-pressure pot-still named 'Ugly Betty', the slow distillation process creates a floral, unique, juniper gin that's mind blowing in a martini.

THE WORLD'S BEST
TONICS
&
MIXERS

Still the way most of us love to imbibe our favourite spirit, gin is perfectly complemented by fresh, prickly tonic water or a craft mixer. Tried and tested, here are world's finest tonics and mixers for your sipping pleasure.

Fever-Tree

This award-winning little British brand took on the big boys and carved a place for itself in the world's finest restaurants, hotels, bars – and bodega shelves. It is made from botanical oils, spring water and the highest quality quinine from the 'fever trees' of the eastern Congo – the ingredient that gives tonic water its slightly bitter edge. Pair it with subtle spirits – artisanal gins packed with heavy juniper notes can become a little overpowering when mixed with a little beauty like this. A drink in its own right.

Fentimans

The 100-year-old artisanal drinks maker's Light and Herbal Tonic Waters are perfect, the latter blended with hyssop and myrtle. But it's their regular Tonic Water, powered with lemongrass, that packs a punch. In the early 1900s, Fentimans sold their beverages (mainly ginger beer) door-to-door in stone jars emblazoned with the company mascot – a dog called Fearless. These days, things are a little different. Fentimans is an international brand with an impressive range of drinks and mixers, alcoholic drinks and one very tasty regular tonic water.

Schweppes

With craft-made, artisanal mixers fast gaining in the tonic market, it's easy to forget about the big boys. Schweppes remains the world's most popular tonic and there's a good reason why: its wonderfully prickly fizz and well-balanced bitter–sweet ratio is completely unique. It's generally considered the bartender's favourite, letting the complex qualities of premium gin sing out loud and proud. So, while the home mixer might fall for new hipster brands, Schweppes is nothing to be sniffed at. The brand's range of premium-flavoured mixers presented in cute lightbulb-shaped bottles is serious competition to the craft mixer gang.

Merchant's Heart

This Willy Wonka-like range of mixers was created with the help of the world's finest bartenders to enhance the spirits they're paired with (not really to be sipped on their own). Hisbiscus, pink peppercorn and floral aromatics all have complex, vivid flavour profiles, but it's MH's Classic Tonic that excites: its sweetness is underlined by a tart and bravely medicinal flavour with deliciously bitter quinine. This delightful, forward-thinking and powerfully fizzy newcomer is from Japanese mega-brand Suntory and is powered by a Bikan Yuso philosophy, translating as 'a sense of beauty and playful imagination'.

Square Root

Square Root Soda, a small batch brand (conceived in a kitchen, sold first at a farmer's market, and now brewed and bottled under a railway in East London), bump up their cultish core collection of sparkling sippers with a host of seasonal, limited-edition flavours from bergamot to rhubarb. Start with the Square's delicious pair of crisp, dry and delicious botanical tonics: Square Root Hop Tonic is powered by Citra and Columbus hops and Sicilian lemon, drawing fresh and fruity tones from gin (imagine an ice-cold shandy without the yeasty edge); it's best with a citrus- or juniper-heavy spirit. Artemisia Tonic is woody and fruity, with a bitter, mineral edge via wormwood, mugwort and tarragon, and best with herby, verdant gins and vodkas. Something rather special.

Indi & Co.

Spanish brand Indi & Co. uses Seville orange peel, Indian kewra (a fragrant, flowery pandanus extract), yuzu from Japan, and calamansi citrus from the Philippines along with quinine and an impossibly laborious process of grinding and distilling (in 200-year-old stills) to create its downright delicious tonic water. Inspired by yesteryear India, birthplace of the quinine tonic, Indi & Co. is carbonated, bottled and (very pleasingly) labelled in Jerez de la Frontera. The brand also creates organic versions of its Classic, Strawberry and Lemon tonics and a Black Kola Nut & Violet mixer that is rich and tasty.

1724

Two fun facts: the first is that the ideal *terroir* for quinine, extracted from the cinchona tree, is 1724 metres (5,656 feet) above sea level. Chilean tonic brand 1724 has mined history to argue that quinine was first discovered on the Inca trail, at high altitude – just where they pluck theirs. Whether or not this affects the mysterious compound is unclear, but 1724 is indeed delicious, perfectly balanced between bitter and sweet tones with a refined, neutral citrus taste designed to let a premium gin shine through. Try with Monkey 47 and a sprig of rosemary for a crisp herbal hit. The other fun fact? Quinine has a fluorescence quantum yield, meaning it glows under ultraviolet light.

Bradley's Kina Tonic

Bradley's Kina Tonic is a modern miracle. A Kickstarter campaign paved the way for Brad (a brewer, distiller and bartender) to create his lauded (and rather old-fashioned) tonic syrup, reinventing the classic Gin and Tonic with natural ingredients and complex flavours. The foundation is Peruvian cinchona (aka Kina) bark, a quinine-rich raw ingredient with a dark, bitter-sweet and earthy edge, and cold-pressed orange oil, which create a cordial-like tonic to add to soda water. The non-sparkling product means Brad can infuse other flavours; his aged bourbon barrel edition has a warm, spiced edge. A perfect tonic syrup; BYO bubbles.

Owen's Craft Mixers

Booze-loving bros (well, bros-in-law, to be exact) Josh Miller and Tyler Holland opened NYC-based Owen's Craft Mixers in 2015. The 'Owen' in question is Josh's entrepreneurial great, great grandfather who ran a general store and bar in Maine, and the pair now make mixers in his name. Their zingy Ginger + Lime and Grapefruit + Lime craft mixers have become something of an indie hit and the Owen's Mega Mule (a giant Moscow Mule served in a bucket-sized copper mug – cue a gazillion Instagram posts) has become an NYC cocktail institution.

Top Note Tonics

Beverage science expert Mary Pellettieri and biz partner created Top Note in 2014, and since then the Milwaukee-based brand has gone from strength to strength. Originally focused on brewing a herbal beer, Pellettieri became interested in the old-style tonics of bar history, created by pharmacists to put lead in your pencil. Their craft mixer range is note-perfect with its Indian Tonic considered the 'IPA of tonics'.

Strangelove

Melbourne: home to the world's highest concentration of hipsters and curious craft mixer brand StrangeLove. The Strange team are onto something: finding the balance between maintaining wellness via an organic, healthy and pure lifestyle with the urge to get eye-crossingly wrecked on a Friday night. The brand design is gorgeous, contemporary with a playfulness, but it's the range that is outstanding in its uniqueness. With Light and Classic tonics and a razor-sharp Bitter Lemon at its core, StrangeLove also offers its infamous Dirty Tonic (a woodier, slightly salty affair), a Blood Orange & Chilli Soda and Smoked Cola.

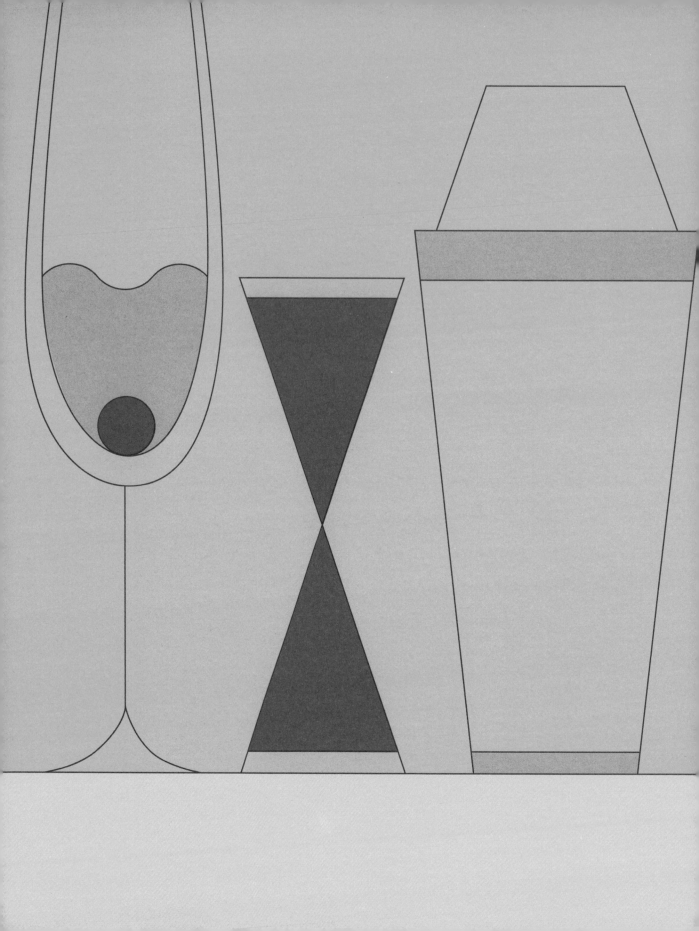

2

The Tool Box

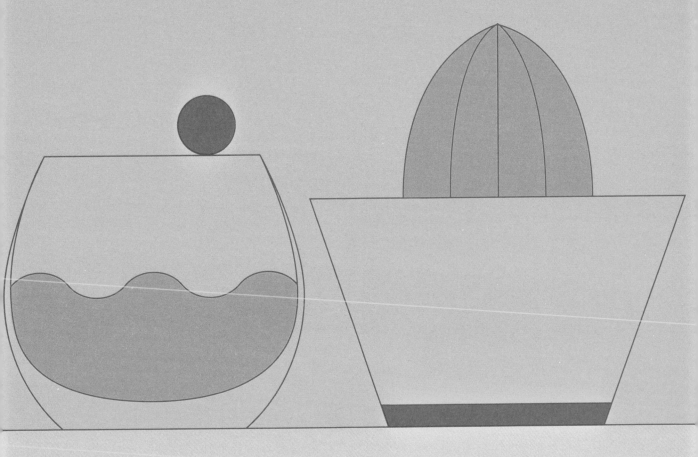

Build up your gin toolbox with this essential cocktail gadgetry, from bar spoons and jiggers to shakers and strainers. No plastic penis straws allowed.

THE
ESSENTIALS

**Start off simple:
a shaker, jigger, blender, strainer and
an ice bucket, and build up from there.**

Jigger

Meet the jigger, the metal, glass or plastic standard measure for spirits and liqueurs, available in many different sizes. Heavy metallic jiggers look the part, but plastic or glass versions also do the job. If you don't have a jigger or single shot glass as a stand-in, use an egg cup – at least then your ratios will be right, even if your shots might be a little under- or over-generous – failing that, cross your fingers, free-pour your drinks, and hope for the best.

Shaker

Aka the Boston shaker, this should be your first purchase. It's a cocktail essential; your single most important piece of kit as very few cocktails are possible without one. The classic metallic model has three main parts: a base, known as the 'can' (a tall, tumbler shape that tapers out), a tight-fitting funnel top with built-in strainer, onto which fits a small cap (that can also be used as a jigger). Invest in a good-quality modern shaker (vintage shakers look amazing but be wary of how effective they are. My 1930s Art Deco silver shaker dribbles like a St Bernard, but it looks the part). The shaker is brilliantly straightforward and, like all the finest tools, it pays to keep it scrupulously clean. If you can't get your hands on one, consider a large glass jar with a lid and waterproof seal.

Mixing Glass

Invest in a simple, sturdy straight-sided glass (also known as the Boston) – or a straight-sided pint glass that tapers out. It's essential for cocktails that need stirring rather than shaking or to allow for extra volume when attached to the can of your shaker (to make two or more drinks at a time). The two halves are locked together and you shake until the drink is chilled, then a Hawthorne strainer can be used to strain the drink.

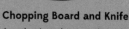

Chopping Board and Knife

A no brainer, but worth adding to your tool kit. Consider a marble or stone board for added slickness, and keep it clean, the knife super sharp and practise your peeling skills: the aim is to avoid as much white pith as possible, leaving just the peel that is studded with aromatic oils.

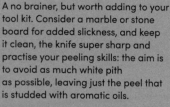

Blender

Essential for slushy, smooth, fruity little numbers. Most domestic blenders find ice a little difficult, so it's best to use crushed ice in blender cocktails, rather than cubes or rocks. Add your ingredients first, then the ice, and start off on a slow speed before turning it up to max. No need to strain. Once the consistency is super-smooth, pour into a glass and serve.

Juicer

It's an investment, sure, but you'll end up with the next level in gin cocktails, and think of all the green juice #cleaneating #blessed Instagram opportunities. Perfect for extracting the pure juice from fruit or ginger root etc – rather than adding the pith, skin, seeds and fibres as with a smoothie.

Ice Bucket

The centrepiece of your home bar; it can be simple, functional and slightly retro or the full plastic pineapple. An insulated ice bucket means your ice cubes will keep their shape for longer, and a good set of vintage tongs adds a touch of class.

Hawthorne Strainer

This rather showy-looking strainer, trimmed with a spring, comes in handy when your shaker's built-in version isn't up to the job. Place on a glass and pour the cocktail through it or hold up against the cocktail can or mixing glass and pour from a height. Make sure you pick a Hawthorne that's compatible with your shaker and always rinse immediately after use, especially if you're straining a cream-based cocktail. A fine tea strainer does the job brilliantly, but the classic Hawthorne does the job and really looks the part.

Citrus Press

A genius little invention and a sturdy alternative to using your hands to squeeze the juice through your fingers, catching the pips as you go. The citrus squeezer is a hand press for all your citrus fruits. Chop the fruit in half, place on the squeezer, then press with all your might as the juice runs out into the bowl and the pips and pith stay behind.

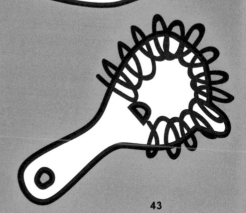

THE LUXURIES

There's something more than a little pleasing about adding the odd frill to your drink, but creating truly delicious cocktails means they should taste and look otherworldly, just as they are.

Cocktail Stick (Toothpick)

For spearing cherries, citrus peel, fruit slices, olives, onion slivers, pickles – sausages, even.

Muddler

A short, usually wooden baton – sometimes with a knobbly rubber tip – used to mash and muddle fruit, herbs, ice and sugar in the glass, bruising and bashing up your ingredients to release their natural oils and flavours. Think of it as a pestle and mortar for your drinks.
If you don't have a muddler, use a flat-ended rolling pin – and a gentle touch.

Ice Pick

In homage to 90s thriller *Basic Instinct*, buy an ice block and invest in an ice pick. Place on a clean dish towel (to steady the block, rather than using your hand), and then attack as needed. The ice will go everywhere, but bear with it. Keep the rocks large and jagged. Make your own home-made ice block by boiling water, letting it cool and pouring into a plastic container (or use premium bottled water). Nineties thriller-inspired erotic stabbing not your thing? Buy in bags of filtered crushed ice or cubes (and always buy double or triple the amount you think you'll need).

Swizzle Stick

Abnormal number of nervous guests? More than just cocktail furniture, the swizzle stick allows the drinker to navigate their own drink, stirring as they go, and fiddling their cares away. Great for drinks packed with fresh fruit and garnishes.

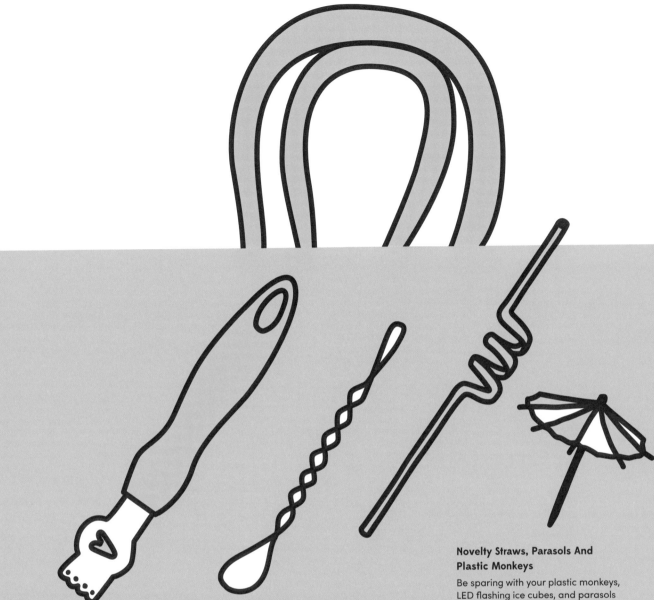

Canele or Julienne Knife

A fancy bit of kit: the canele knife has a V-shaped groove for cutting citrus peel spirals, carving melons and probably many other crafty uses.

Bar Spoon

It's not essential, but looks pretty cool in your cocktail kit line-up. The classic bar spoon has a long, twisted handle, a flat end and a teardrop-shaped spoon used for stirring and measuring out ingredients.

Novelty Straws, Parasols And Plastic Monkeys

Be sparing with your plastic monkeys, LED flashing ice cubes, and parasols stick to paper straws wherever you can (think of the oceans!) and save your penis straws for extra special occasions (80th birthday parties).

A GUIDE TO
GLASSES

Using the right type of glass is a must. Each cocktail has its perfect glass to show off its colour and tone, to keep it cooler for longer or simply to stand out from the crowd.

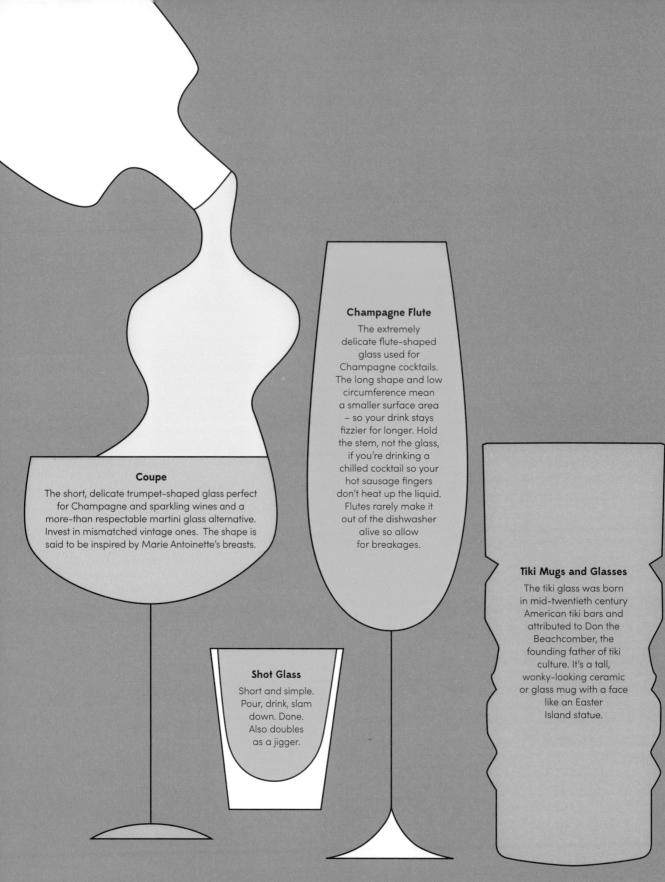

Coupe

The short, delicate trumpet-shaped glass perfect for Champagne and sparkling wines and a more-than respectable martini glass alternative. Invest in mismatched vintage ones. The shape is said to be inspired by Marie Antoinette's breasts.

Champagne Flute

The extremely delicate flute-shaped glass used for Champagne cocktails. The long shape and low circumference mean a smaller surface area – so your drink stays fizzier for longer. Hold the stem, not the glass, if you're drinking a chilled cocktail so your hot sausage fingers don't heat up the liquid. Flutes rarely make it out of the dishwasher alive so allow for breakages.

Tiki Mugs and Glasses

The tiki glass was born in mid-twentieth century American tiki bars and attributed to Don the Beachcomber, the founding father of tiki culture. It's a tall, wonky-looking ceramic or glass mug with a face like an Easter Island statue.

Shot Glass

Short and simple. Pour, drink, slam down. Done. Also doubles as a jigger.

Martini

The iconic glass has a refined stem and cone-shape that flares out to create a shallow recess. Somehow it loses its ability not to slosh out its contents as the evening wears on, so switch to clear spirits when you're half cut.

Collins Glass

The skinnier, lither little sister of the Highball, usually with straight sides and a delicate countenance.

Jam Jar

There are no hard-and-fast rules for how you serve your drinks – or what you serve them in. You can use any number of alternatives – jam jars, tea cups, sciencey test tubes and beakers, Russian tea glasses, sippy cups, shoes – to get your guests beyond the pale.

Highball

Ostensibly a tall glass, with a thick and sturdy bottom, that holds 225–350 ml (8–12 oz) of perfectly mixed booze.

Boston Glass

The twin brother of the straight-sided pint glass, swapped at birth. Great for mixing in or for using locked into the can of your shaker.

Tumbler

The short, straight-sided glass perfect for short or single shot drinks. Like most things, best to pick one with a nice, chunky bottom.

COCKTAIL TRICKS

There's more to making a gin cocktail than grabbing a shaker and furiously bashing one out. It's not what you have, it's what you do with it.

Shake It Off

How long exactly to shake the perfect concoction? No one can agree. Some say 15 seconds of brisk shaking, others say less. Best to sit on the fence and opt for a short and sharp 7 seconds or so. Any longer could dilute the drink a little too much, affecting its potency. Otherwise, there should be no bottle flipping or sparkler lighting, although a little lemon and lime juggling wouldn't go amiss.

Stirrers

Whip out your bar spoon and your mixing glass, and stir drinks gently and deftly with ice to chill the concoction. You'll know when it's ready when condensation forms on the outside of the glass.

Be Chill

If you have room, clear a shelf in your freezer and keep your cocktail glasses on ice, or pack them full of cubes to throw away when the glass is chilled. There's little more thirst-quenching than a frosty-looking chilled glass filled with your favourite G & T.

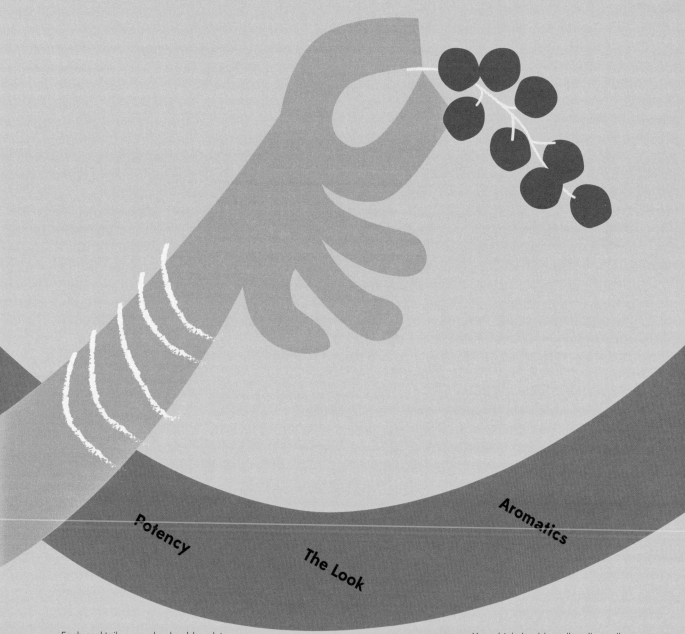

Potency

The Look

Aromatics

Each cocktail you make should seek to achieve a perfect balance of flavours and, although certain drinks might attempt differing levels of intensity, it shouldn't get you drunk – at least not on its own. Perfect measurements really do matter. The perfect cocktail doesn't have to make your lips numb.

Fresher than fresh garnishes, squeaky clean and chilled glasses, purified ice, sturdy gadgets and a perfect balance of colours and visible textures are essential.

Your drink should smell really, really great – not just taste good. Bitters, fresh juices and citrus peels packed with fragrant oils help to achieve this. Twisting a fresh and floppy citrus peel over a drink before serving is a perfect way to pep-up your presentation.

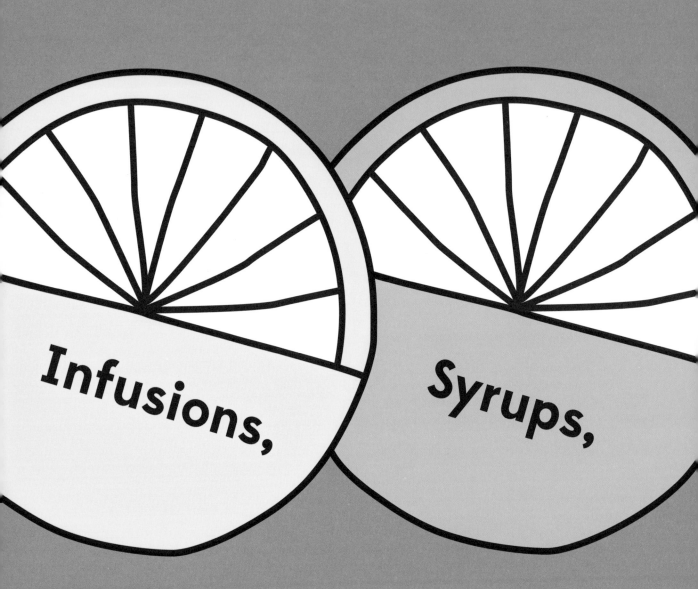

3

Infusions, Syrups,

Turn the toughest liquor into soda pop with the sweet stuff: aromatic syrups and reductions that'll transform your cocktail-making.

Sours and Brines

INFUSIONS

Super-charge your favourite gin with your own hand-picked infusions to create a power-punch of flavour.

Sloe Gin

Place 500 g (1 lb 2 oz) freshly picked sloes into a large bowl of water with 1 teaspoon salt for 20 minutes (this will remove any unwanted guests!)

Rinse in clean water and pat dry. Using the tip of a sharp knife, prick the sloes all over. Drop into a large sterilised preserving jar (see page 55), add 250 g (9 oz) caster (superfine) sugar and 1 litre (34 oz) gin, then seal tightly. Shake well every day for a week or so, then place in a cool and dark place for 8–12 weeks.

After this time, line a funnel with a muslin (cheesecloth) or a coffee filter. Decant into clean and sterilised bottles (see page 55). Seal tightly. The gin is now ready to be used or you can store it for up to a year if you want the flavour to mature.

Sloe & Star Anise Gin

Add a handful of freshly picked sloes into a large bowl of water with 1 teaspoon salt for 20 minutes. Rinse in clean water and pat dry. Using the tip of a sharp knife or a cocktail stick, prick the sloes all over and add them to 500 ml (17 oz) gin along with a single star anise pod, bashed into manageable pieces, and 1 teaspoon of brown sugar. Let it steep for at least 3 days in a cool, dark place before straining and serving. Store for up to 6 weeks in the fridge in the original bottle.

Rhubarb Gin

Cut 1 kg (2 lb 3 oz) rhubarb (shed-grown 'forced' rhubarb will give a much more vibrant pink colour) into 2.5 cm (1 inch) pieces and combine with 500 g (1 lb 2 oz) caster (superfine) sugar in a large sterilised preserving jar (see page 55). Shake well, seal and leave overnight at room temperature. Add 1 litre (34 oz) gin and shake. Leave to cool in a dark place for 8–12 weeks.

Line a funnel with a muslin (cheesecloth) or a coffee filter and decant the gin into clean and sterilised bottles (see page 55) and seal tightly.

You can also omit the decanting stage, and use straight from the jar, fruit and all.

Bay Leaf Gin

Use 2–3 fresh bay leaves per 500 ml (17 oz) gin. Let it steep for at least 3 days in a cool, dark place before straining and serving. Store for up to 6 weeks in the fridge in the original bottle. Otherworldly in a Bay Leaf & Green Tea Martini (see page 104).

Lavender Gin

Add 6 lavender sprigs to 1 litre (32 oz) gin in a large sterilised preserving jar and seal tightly. Store at room temperature for 2–5 days (depending on the freshness of the lavender and how much flavour you require – feel free to check daily).

Line a funnel with a muslin (cheesecloth) or a coffee filter, decant into clean and sterilised bottles (see below) and seal tightly. You can garnish the jar by dropping in a final sprig of lavender.

TIP
Sterilise jars by washing them thoroughly and placing in the oven at 180°C (350°F/Gas 4) for 10 minutes. To sterilise the lids or seals, just boil in water for 10 minutes. Or more simply, put the jars, lids and seals through a dishwasher on a hot cycle. If you're adding cold liquid, allow the jars to cool first.

Ginger Gin

This fiery infusion creates a rather spicy note. Add a thumb-sized, peeled piece of fresh ginger to 500 ml (17 oz) gin. Let it steep for at least 3 days in a cool, dark place before straining and removing the ginger. Store for up to 6 weeks in the fridge.

SYRUPS & REDUCTIONS

Turn the toughest liquor into soda pop with the sweet stuff: aromatic syrups and reductions that'll transform your cocktail-making.

Tempranillo Reduction

Makes enough dashes for approximately 15 drinks

tempranillo wine	200 ml (7 oz)
crushed star anise	a pinch
dark brown sugar	100 g (3½ oz)
corn syrup or golden syrup (optional)	1 tbsp

Simmer the wine and star anise in a non-stick saucepan and gently add the sugar. Turn down the heat and stir constantly with a wooden spoon for 3–5 minutes, until all the sugar has dissolved and the mixture has reduced by approximately one-third. Turn off the heat and leave to cool for 20–30 minutes for the flavours to infuse. While still runny, decant into a sterilised preserving jar, or funnel into a sterilised glass bottle with a stopper (see page 55). Adding a spoonful of syrup to the cooled mixture now will help keep the reduction smooth. Store in the fridge for up to 6 weeks.

Equipment

Non-stick saucepan, wooden spoon, 200 ml (7 oz) preserving jar or glass bottle with stopper, funnel

Lavender & Rose Syrup

Makes enough dashes for approximately 15 drinks

water	200 ml (6½ oz)
caster (superfine) sugar	400 g (13 oz)
lavender buds	2 tablespoons
dried rose petals	10 g (½ oz)
water	200 ml (6½ oz)

Combine the water and sugar in a heavy bottomed saucepan. Bring to a gentle boil, stirring to ensure sugar has fully dissolved. Add the lavendar buds and rose petals and simmer for about 8–10 minutes. Take it off the heat and leave to steep for at least 4 hours and cool completely.

Strain through a funnel lined with a muslin (cheesecloth) or a coffee filter into a sterilised jar or bottle (see page 55) and store.

Equipment

Heavy-based pan, funnel, muslin (cheesecloth) or a coffee filter, a sterilised bottle

Simple Syrup

Makes enough dashes for approximately 15 drinks

water	200 ml (7 oz)
unrefined demerara, cane or granulated (raw) sugar	100 g (3½ oz)
corn syrup or golden syrup (optional)	1 tbsp

Boil the water in a non-stick saucepan and gently add the sugar. Turn down the heat and stir constantly with a wooden spoon for 3–5 minutes, until all the sugar has dissolved and the syrup is clear. Turn off the heat and leave to cool. While still runny, pour into a sterilised preserving jar, or funnel into a sterilised glass bottle with a stopper (see page 55). Adding a spoonful of syrup to the cooled mixture will help keep the syrup smooth. Store in the fridge for up to 6 weeks.

Equipment

Non-stick saucepan, wooden spoon, 200 ml (7 oz) preserving jar or glass bottle with a stopper, funnel

Rhubarb, Ginger & Star Anise Syrup

Makes enough dashes for approximately 15 drinks

water	200 ml (7 oz)
unrefined demerara, cane or granulated (raw) sugar	100 g (3½ oz)
rhubarb stalks, cut into chunks	2
grated fresh ginger	1 tbsp
star anise, slightly crushed	1
freshly squeezed lemon juice	a dash
corn syrup or golden syrup (optional)	1 tbsp

Boil the water in a non-stick saucepan and gently add the sugar, rhubarb, ginger, star anise and lemon juice. Turn down the heat and stir constantly with a wooden spoon for 3–5 minutes until all the sugar has dissolved. Turn off the heat and leave to cool for 20–30 minutes. While still runny, pass through a strainer lined with a muslin (cheesecloth) or a coffee filter into a heatproof bowl, then decant into a sterilised preserving jar or funnel into a sterilised glass bottle with stopper (see page 55). Adding a spoonful of syrup will help keep the mixture smooth. Store in the fridge for up to 6 weeks.

Equipment

Non-stick saucepan, wooden spoon, muslin (cheesecloth) or a coffee filter, heatproof bowl, 200 ml (7 oz) preserving jar or glass bottle with stopper, funnel

Cornflower or Borage Syrup

Makes enough dashes for approximately 15 drinks

water	200 ml (7 oz)
caster (superfine) sugar	200 g (7 oz)
cornflowers or borage	a handful

Combine the water and sugar in a heavy-based saucepan. Bring to a gentle boil, stirring to ensure the sugar has fully dissolved. Add the flowers and boil for another minute. Take off the heat and leave to steep for at least 4 hours and cool completely. Strain through a funnel lined with a muslin (or a coffee filter) into a sterilised jar or bottle (see page 55) and store.

Equipment

Heavy-based saucepan, funnel, muslin (cheesecloth) or a coffee filter, preserving jar or bottle

Spiced Brown Sugar Syrup

Makes enough dashes for approximately 15 drinks

water	200 ml (7 oz)
unrefined dark brown sugar	100 g (3½ oz)
grated fresh ginger	1 tbsp
corn syrup or golden syrup (optional)	1 tbsp

Boil the water in a non-stick saucepan and gently add the sugar and ginger. Turn down the heat and stir constantly with a wooden spoon for 3–5 minutes, until all the sugar has dissolved. Turn off the heat and leave to cool for 20–30 minutes for the flavours to infuse. While still runny, pass through a strainer lined with a muslin (cheesecloth) or a coffee filter into a heatproof bowl, then decant into a sterilised preserving jar or funnel into a sterilised glass bottle with a stopper (see page 55). Adding a spoonful of syrup to the cooled mixture now will help keep the syrup smooth. Store in the fridge for up to 6 weeks.

Equipment

Non-stick saucepan, wooden spoon, muslin (cheesecloth) or a coffee filter, heatproof bowl, 200 ml (7 oz) preserving jar or glass bottle with stopper, funnel

Cherry & Thyme Syrup

Pine Tip Syrup

Makes enough dashes for approximately 15 drinks

water	200 ml (7 oz)
unrefined demerara, cane or granulated (raw) sugar	100 g (3½ oz)
ripe, squishy cherries, stoned	a handful
large thyme sprig	1
corn syrup or golden syrup (optional)	1 tbsp

Boil the water in a non-stick saucepan and gently add the sugar, cherries and thyme. Turn down the heat and stir constantly for 3–5 minutes until all the sugar has dissolved. Turn off the heat and leave to cool. While still runny, pour into a sterilised preserving jar or funnel into a sterilised glass bottle with a stopper (see page 55). Adding a spoonful of syrup to the cooled mixture will help keep the syrup smooth. Store in the fridge for up to 6 weeks.

Equipment

Non-stick saucepan, wooden spoon, 200 ml (7 oz) preserving jar or glass bottle with stopper, funnel

Makes enough dashes for approximately 15 drinks

water	200 ml (7 oz)
unrefined demerara, cane or granulated (raw) sugar	100 g (3½ oz)
freshly picked pine tips (the bright green leaves from spruce or pine trees, rather than the dark green, older leaves)	a handful
corn syrup or golden syrup (optional)	1 tbsp

Boil the water in a non-stick saucepan and gently add the sugar and pine tips. Turn down the heat and stir constantly with a wooden spoon for 3–5 minutes until all the sugar has dissolved and the syrup is clear. Turn off the heat and leave to cool. While still runny, pour into a sterilised preserving jar or funnel into a sterilised glass bottle with a stopper (see page 55). Adding a spoonful of syrup to the cooled mixture will help keep the syrup smooth. Store in the fridge for up to 6 weeks.

Equipment

Non-stick saucepan, wooden spoon, 200 ml (7 oz) preserving jar or glass bottle with a stopper, funnel

Other Flavoured Syrups

Using Simple Syrup (see page 58) as the base, make your own infusions, tweaking amounts to taste according to the potency of your flavourings. A sprig or two for rosemary syrup should do it, whereas mint syrup needs a good handful. It's not an exact science.

Brown Sugar & Molasses

Basil & Lime

Cinnamon

Elderflower

Ground Coffee

Honey

Mint

Pink Peppercorn

Rhubarb

Rosemary

Sage

Vanilla Bean

SOURS

Sours – a citrus-based mix that can include sugar syrup and egg white – cut through the gloopy sweetness of liqueurs. Shaken up with egg white and sugar syrup, a hit of fresh lemon and lime juice, or grapefruit and blood orange, is the fizzing topnote of recipes like the Classic Sour. But a simple half-measure of lemon juice stirred through any sweet concoction will also do the trick, turning a grandma's snifter into something otherworldly.

Simple Sour Mix

freshly squeezed lemon juice	15 ml (½ oz)
freshly squeezed lime juice	15 ml (½ oz)

Mix both juices and deploy.

Classic Sour Mix

freshly squeezed lemon juice	15 ml (½ oz)
freshly squeezed lime juice	15 ml (½ oz)
Simple Syrup (see page 58)	15 ml (½ oz)
egg white	1

Mix both juices, the sugar syrup and egg white together and shake over ice with your chosen spirit.

Equipment
Shaker

Bloody Sour Mix

freshly squeezed blood orange juice	15 ml (½ oz)
freshly squeezed pink grapefruit juice	15 ml (½ oz)

Mix both juices and deploy.

BRINES

Olive brine mixed with a gin martini lends a deep, savoury kick; cocktail onions and a drop of vinegar add a sharp, acrid note, and a drop of pickle juice seems only to increase gin's firepower. The best bit? It's like having a drink and dinner in one, which, frankly, allows time for more drinking. There are no precise instructions or quantities here – add your choice of brine stolen from olive, caper and pickle jars – according to taste.

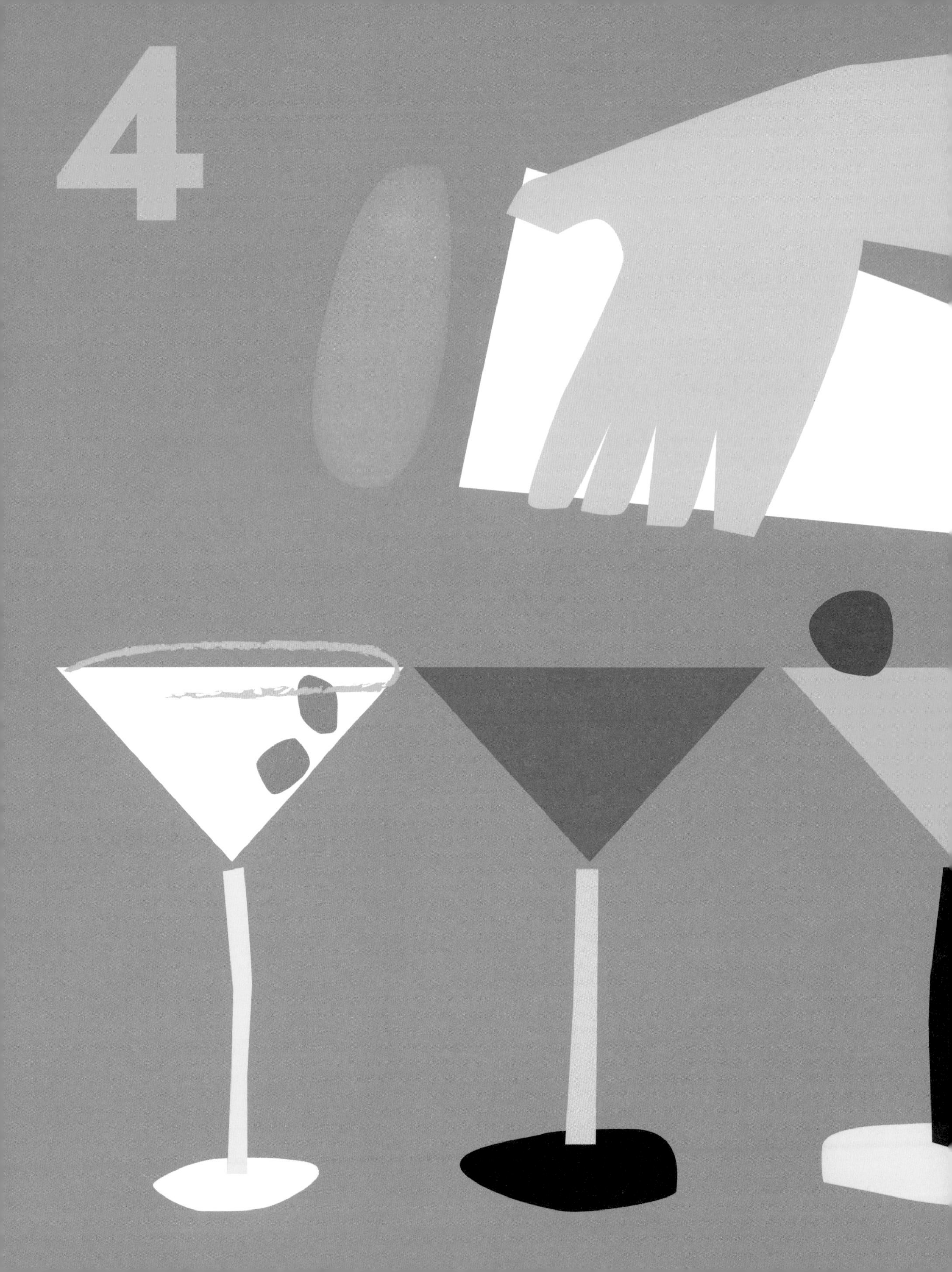

From zingy classics to contemporary upstarts sizzling with flavour – and a few cucumber-shaped surprises – get ready to shake, muddle and stir.

RECIPES

THE CLASSICS

The most enduring (and ridiculously tasty) cocktails of
gin history: master the recipes that have made
the great and good tipsy for decades.

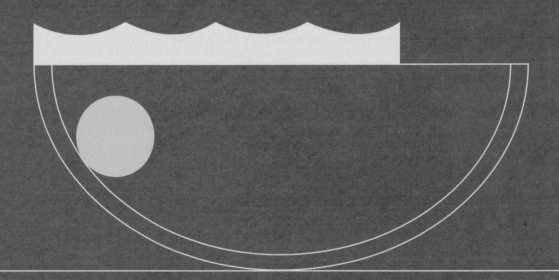

GLASSWARE

Highball

GARNISH

Cucumber spear

EQUIPMENT

Bar spoon   **Strainer**

GLASSWARE

Coupe

GARNISH

Lemon twist

EQUIPMENT

Boston glass or shaker

Bar spoon   **Strainer**

Perfect G & T

gin	60 ml (2 oz)
freshly squeezed lime juice	a splash
premium tonic water	to top up
orange bitters	a dash

Add the gin, lime juice and cucumber spear to a chilled glass filled with ice cubes and stir with a spoon. Top with chilled premium tonic and a dash of orange bitters. Garnish with a cucumber spear and serve with a straw.

TIP
Run a wedge of lime around the rim of the glass for extra limey-ness.

Pink Gin

gin (ideally Plymouth Gin)	60 ml (2 oz)
Angostura bitters	a dash

Add the gin and Angostura bitters to a Boston glass or shaker filled with ice. Stir with a long bar spoon to combine. Strain into a chilled glass and garnish with a lemon twist (see page 95). See photo opposite.

TIP
Originally invented by the navy as a medicinal drink for sailors. The stronger the proof of gin you use, the more you'll want to dilute it by stirring for longer. This is the best cocktail if you want to test craft gin brands as it's clean and lets the gin's flavours come through.

The Classics

Tom Collins

Highball

Lemon wedge

Bar spoon

gin (ideally Old Tom)	45 ml (1½ oz)
freshly squeezed lemon juice	30 ml (1 oz)
Simple Syrup (see page 58)	22½ ml (¾ oz)
soda water	to top up

Fill a chilled glass with ice, add the gin, lemon juice and simple syrup and stir. Top with soda and stir once to combine. Squeeze a lemon wedge over the drink and drop into the glass to garnish.

Singapore Sling

gin	45 ml (1½ oz)
cherry brandy	15 ml (½ oz)
Cointreau or orange liqueur	7½ ml (¼ oz)
Bénédictine or herbal liqueur	7½ ml (¼ oz)
pineapple juice	120 ml (4 oz)
freshly squeezed lime juice	15 ml (½ oz)
grenadine	7½ ml (¼ oz)
Angostura bitters	a dash

Add all of the ingredients to a cocktail shaker filled with ice. Shake vigorously until well chilled and then strain into a chilled glass filled with ice. Garnish with a speared cherry and pineapple wedge.

Bramble

Tumbler or highball

GARNISH

Fresh blackberries

Mint sprig

EQUIPMENT

Muddler

fresh blackberries	a handful
gin	60 ml (2 oz)
freshly squeezed lemon juice	15 ml (½ oz)
Simple Syrup (see page 58)	splash
crème de mûre	splash

Gently muddle the handful of fresh blackberries with the gin, lemon juice and syrup in a chilled glass. Add crushed ice and a generous splash of crème de mûre. Garnish with fresh blackberries and mint.

TIP
Forage for the blackberries yourself – it will taste 100 per cent more amazing.

Salty Dog
(straight up)

Coupe

Sea salt rim

Saucer to salt rim

Shaker

Strainer

gin	45 ml (1½ oz)
freshly squeezed grapefruit juice	60 ml (2 oz)
Simple Syrup (see page 58)	7½ ml (¼ oz)
rhubarb bitters	2 dashes

Place all of the ingredients into a cocktail shaker filled with ice.
Shake hard, then strain into a chilled, salt-rimmed glass. For the salt rim,
squish a lime wedge along the edge of a chilled glass and dip in sea salt.

Floradora

gin	45 ml (1½ oz)
Chambord or any brand of crème de framboise	15 ml (½ oz)
freshly squeezed lemon juice	15 ml (½ oz)
Ginger ale	to top up

Fill a tall, chilled glass with ice and add the gin, Chambord and lemon juice. Top up with ginger ale and stir once to combine. Drop the garnish straight into the cocktail.

TIP
Impress your friends with this fun fact: the Floradora is named after a comedy musical from the early 1900s.

GLASSWARE

Collins

GARNISH

Speared lime

Raspberry

EQUIPMENT

Bar spoon

Aviation

gin	60 ml (2 oz)
maraschino liqueur	7½ ml (¼ oz)
Crème de violette	7½ ml (¼ oz)
freshly squeezed lemon juice	15 ml (½ oz)

Add all of the ingredients to a Boston glass or shaker filled with ice. Shake until chilled, then strain into a chilled glass. Warm a piece of lemon zest over a lighter or small flame, squeeze over the drink and drop in.

Gin Buck

lemon	½
gin	60 ml (2 oz)
ginger ale	to top up

Fill a chilled glass with ice and squeeze over the juice of ½ lemon. Add the gin and top up with ginger ale. Stir once to combine and garnish with a wedge of lemon.

TIP
You can swap the lemon juice for lime juice for less than a sharp 'Buck.

GLASSWARE

Collins

GARNISH

Lemon wedge

EQUIPMENT

Bar spoon

Long Island Iced Tea

Highball

Lemon

Lime slices

Bar spoon

gin	30 ml (1 oz)
vodka	30 ml (1 oz)
light rum	30 ml (1 oz)
tequila	30 ml (1 oz)
freshly squeezed lemon juice	30 ml (1 oz)
orange liqueur	30 ml (1 oz)
cola	a splash

Pour the ingredients into a chilled glass filled with ice cubes. Stir a the spoon and add the citrus slices. Serve with a straw.

The Classics

Clover Club

Coupe

**Three speared
raspberries**

Shaker   **Strainer**

gin	45 ml (1½ oz)
freshly squeezed lemon juice	30 ml (1 oz)
raspberry purée	30 ml (1 oz)
Simple Syrup (see page 58)	15 ml (½ oz)
egg white	1

Add all of the ingredients to a cocktail shaker and dry shake without ice.
Fill the shaker with ice and shake again until cold. Strain into a chilled glass
and garnish with fresh raspberries.

TIP
*To dry shake: first shake the ingredients without ice, then add ice and
shake again.*

Monkey Gland

gin	60 ml (2 oz)
freshly squeezed orange juice	30 ml (1 oz)
grenadine	7½ ml (¼ oz)
absinthe	2 dashes

Place all of the ingredients into a cocktail shaker filled with ice and shake vigorously. Strain into a chilled glass and garnish with an orange twist (see page 95).

TIP
Created by Harry MacElhone of Harry's New York Bar in Paris. Quite what he was doing with monkey glands we'll never know.

GLASSWARE

Martini

GARNISH

Orange twist

EQUIPMENT

Shaker   **Strainer**

Negroni

GLASSWARE

Tumbler

GARNISH

Orange peel twist

EQUIPMENT

Mixing glass   **Strainer**

gin	30 ml (1 oz)
sweet vermouth	30 ml (1 oz)
Campari	60 ml (2 oz)

Stir the gin, vermouth and Campari in a mixing glass over ice. Strain into a glass over a block of ice. Garnish with a twist of orange peel (see page 95).

TIP
Use big, jagged blocks of ice and an over-sized peel twist for extra chill and aromatics.

The Southside

mint sprigs	2–3
gin	60 ml (2 oz)
freshly squeezed lime juice	30 ml (1 oz)
Simple Syrup (see page 58)	15 ml (½ oz)

Softly bruise the mint using a muddler. Shake the ingredients over ice and strain into a chilled glass. Garnish with a fresh mint sprig.

TIP

Dress like a 1930s mobster before you take your first sip.

GLASSWARE

Coupe or martini

GARNISH

Mint sprig

EQUIPMENT

Muddler

Shaker   **Strainer**

Bronx

Martini

Orange twist

Shaker   **Strainer**

gin	45 ml (1½ oz)
sweet vermouth	7½ ml (¼ oz)
dry vermouth	7½ ml (¼ oz)
freshly squeezed orange juice	30 ml (1 oz)

Place all of the ingredients into a cocktail shaker filled with ice. Shake hard to combine, then strain into a chilled glass. Garnish with a twist of orange peel (see page 95).

TIP
This cocktail was named after the birthplace of hip hop, because why not?

Boston Tea Party

gin	15 ml (½ oz)
vodka	15 ml (½ oz)
gold rum	15 ml (½ oz)
Grand Marnier	7½ ml (¼ oz)
Tia Maria	7½ ml (¼ oz)
shop-bought sweet and sour mix	60 ml (2 oz)
cola	to top up

Add the gin, vodka, rum, Grand Marnier, Tia Maria and sweet and sour mix into a cocktail shaker filled with ice. Shake hard to combine until it has a frothy head, then strain into a chilled glass filled with fresh ice. Top up with cola and stir. Squeeze a wedge of lemon over and drop into the drink.

GLASSWARE

Collins

GARNISH

Lemon wedge

EQUIPMENT

Shaker

Strainer   Bar spoon

THE MARTINIS

Gin, vermouth, a chilled glass, and a wry smile: the Martini is one of the purest, most perfect ways to drink gin. Discover the recipes inspired by this potent classic.

Martini

GARNISH

**Speared olive or
a lemon twist**

EQUIPMENT

Boston glass or shaker

Bar spoon   **Strainer**

GLASSWARE

Martini

GARNISH

Olives

EQUIPMENT

Shaker

Bar spoon   **Strainer**

Classic Gin Martini
(Straight Up)

gin	60 ml (2 oz)
dry vermouth	15 ml (½ oz)

Add the gin and vermouth to a Boston glass or shaker filled with ice. Stir with a long bar spoon to combine. Strain into a chilled glass and garnish with an olive or lemon twist (see page 95).

TIPS
Pack in a lot of ice to the mixing glass. Too little ice and you'll end up with wet ice, which will over dilute the drink.

Stirring the drink rather than shaking allows you to control the level of dilution.

Dirty Martini

gin	60 ml (2 oz)
dry vermouth	30 ml (1 oz)
olive brine	to taste

Shake the gin and vermouth over ice, strain and pour into a chilled glass. Spoon in the brine and add an olive or two. See photo opposite.

TIPS
Swap out the olives for caperberries, cocktail onions – even cornichons, if you're that way inclined.

The Martinis

Martinez

Martini

GARNISH

Lemon twist

EQUIPMENT

Boston glass or shaker

Bar spoon   **Strainer**

gin (ideally Old Tom)	60 ml (2 oz)
sweet vermouth	22½ ml (¾ oz)
maraschino liqueur	7½ ml (¼ oz)
Angostura bitters	a dash

Add all of the ingredients to a Boston glass or shaker filled with ice. Stir with a long bar spoon to combine and chill. Strain into a chilled glass and garnish with a twist of lemon.

TIP

The precursor to the classic martini; often known as the 'Father of the Martini'.

The Vesper

gin	60 ml (2 oz)
vodka	30 ml (1 oz)
Lillet Blanc vermouth	15 ml (½ oz)

Add all of the ingredients to a cocktail shaker filled with ice. Shake to chill, then strain into a chilled glass. Garnish with lemon zest.

TIP
This is a fictional drink created by Ian Fleming. Shaking the drink will chill it faster and, as there's quite a lot of alcohol, it also helps to dilute it down.

GLASSWARE

Martini

GARNISH

Lemon zest

EQUIPMENT

Strainer   **Bar spoon**

Gimlet

Coupe or martini

Lime twist

Shaker

Strainer

gin	60 ml (2 oz)
freshly squeezed lime juice	15 ml (½ oz)

Shake the ingredients with ice and vigour, then strain into a chilled glass with a couple of ice cubes. Garnish with a twist of lime.

TIP
Add a little simple or agave syrup if you're sprouting hairs on your chest.

The Martinis

The Gibson

Coupe or martini

Cocktail onions

Shaker

Strainer

gin	60 ml (2 oz)
dry vermouth	15 ml (½ oz)

Shake the gin and dry vermouth over ice, pour into a chilled glass and add 2–3 cocktail onions.

TIP
Chill the glass to make sure the Gibson is served ice cold – don't worry about calories. With the onions, it's practically a salad.

Tuxedo
(No. 2)

gin	60 ml (2 oz)
dry vermouth	22½ ml (¾ oz)
maraschino liqueur	15 ml (½ oz)
orange bitters	2 dashes
absinthe	a dash

Pour the absinthe into a chilled glass, swirl around to coat the inside and then discard. Add the remaining ingredients to a Boston glass or shaker filled with ice and stir until chilled. Strain into the prepared glass and garnish with a lemon twist.

TIP
There are plenty of YouTube videos on how to make lemon twists. My preferred method is to hollow out a lemon, discard the centre (you can juice it and use the juice), keep the skin and cut down one side. Flatten and remove the pith, role into a sausage and then cut up into slices. Place a damp piece of kitchen paper over the top of the curls and they will last all day in the fridge.

GLASSWARE

Martini

GARNISH

Lemon twist

EQUIPMENT

Boston glass or shaker

Bar spoon   **Strainer**

Cornflower Martini

gin	60 ml (2 oz)
dry vermouth	15 ml (½ oz)
Cornflower Syrup (see page 59)	15 ml (½ oz)
freshly squeezed lemon juice	30 ml (1 oz)
egg white	1

Place all of the ingredients into a Boston glass or shaker filled with ice. Shake vigorously to combine and chill. Strain into a chilled glass and garnish with fresh or dried cornflower petals. See photo opposite.

GLASSWARE

Coupe

GARNISH

A fresh cornflower or dried cornflower petals

EQUIPMENT

Boston glass or shaker   **Strainer**

Elderflower Martini

gin	30 ml (1 oz)
vodka	30 ml (1 oz)
St-Germain	30 ml (1 oz)
freshly squeezed lemon juice	15 ml (½ oz)

Shake the wet ingredients over ice, then strain into a chilled glass. Garnish with a mint sprig.

TIP
Add a dash of mint syrup or Simple Syrup (see page 58), to taste.

GLASSWARE

Martini or coupe

GARNISH

Mint sprig

EQUIPMENT

Shaker   **Strainer**

Park Avenue Martini

Coupe or martini

Cherry spear

Shaker

Strainer

gin	60 ml (2 oz)
sweet vermouth	15 ml (½ oz)
triple sec	15 ml (½ oz)
freshly pressed pineapple juice	30 ml (1 oz)
orange bitters	a dash

Add all of the ingredients to a shaker filled with ice. Shake well to combine and chill the drink. Strain into a chilled glass and garnish with a cherry spear.

TIP
Sip with one hand and hail a yellow taxi with the other.

French Martini

gin	60 ml (2 oz)
Chambord	15 ml (½ oz)
freshly pressed pineapple juice	30 ml (1 oz)

Add all of the ingredients to a shaker filled with ice and shake vigorously until chilled. Strain into a chilled glass and top with raspberries.

TIP

This drink can be made with gin or vodka. Using gin makes a slightly drier drink. Must only be drunk wearing a beret.

GLASSWARE

Coupe

GARNISH

Fresh raspberries

EQUIPMENT

Shaker

Strainer

Bergamot Tea Martini

gin	30 ml (1 oz)
vodka	30 ml (1 oz)
premium Earl Grey tea bag	1
orange bitters	a dash

Pour the gin and vodka over a premium Earl Grey tea bag at room temperature. Allow to steep for at least 30 minutes, then remove the tea bag. Add the bitters, shake vigorously over ice, then serve in a chilled glass with orange peel to garnish (see page 95).

GLASSWARE

Tiki or glass mug

GARNISH

Orange peel

EQUIPMENT

Shaker

Lychee Martini

gin	60 ml (2 oz)
lychee purée	45 ml (1½ oz)
dry vermouth	a dash

Place all of the ingredients into a Boston glass or shaker filled with ice. Stir to chill and combine. Place a lychee in the bottom of a chilled glass and strain the drink over the top.

GLASSWARE

Coupe

GARNISH

Lychee

EQUIPMENT

Boston glass or shaker

Bar spoon   **Strainer**

Lavender Martini

Lavender Gin (see page 55)	60 ml (2 oz)
dry vermouth	15 ml (½ oz)
Simple Syrup (see page 58)	15 ml (½ oz)
orange bitters	a dash

Add all of the ingredients to a Boston glass or shaker filled with ice and stir until combined and chilled. Strain into a chilled glass and garnish with a sprig of lavender.

GLASSWARE

Martini

GARNISH

Lavender sprig

EQUIPMENT

Boston glass or shaker

Bar spoon   Strainer

Bay Leaf & Green Tea Martini

GLASSWARE

Martini or Coupe or Tumbler

GARNISH

Fresh bay leaf

EQUIPMENT

Shaker

Strainer

premium green tea bag	1
vodka	30 ml (1 oz)
Bay Leaf Gin (see page 55)	60 ml (2 oz)
freshly squeezed lemon juice	15 ml (½ oz)

Steep the tea tea bag in the vodka and at room temperature for 30 minutes. Remove the tea bag. Shake the wet ingredients over ice, then strain into a chilled glass. Top with the lemon juice and garnish with a fresh bay leaf.

TIP
Add a dash of Simple Syrup (see page 58) to taste.

The Martinis

Behind every great cocktail is a powerful, premium spirit desperate to make itself known. These recipes bring gin out into the spotlight.

GIN-FOCUSED

COCKTAILS

Saketini

Cocktail

Maraschino cherries

Boston glass or shaker

Bar spoon

gin (ideally a London Dry)	60 ml (2 oz)
sake	15 ml (½ oz)
maraschino liqueur	7½ ml (1¼ oz)

Pour all of the ingredients into a Boston glass or shaker filled with ice. Stir with a long bar spoon to combine and chill. Strain into a chilled glass and garnish with a maraschino cherry or two.

Green Dragon

gin	60 ml (2 oz)
green crème de menthe	15 ml (½ oz)
freshly squeezed lime juice	15 ml (½ oz)
Angostura bitters	2 dashes

Place all of the Ingredients into a cocktail shaker filled with ice and shake hard to chill. Strain into a chilled glass and garnish with a mint sprig.

Tip
Dresscode for this drink: Khaleesi

GLASSWARE

Martini

GARNISH

Mint sprig

EQUIPMENT

Shaker

Strainer

British Summer Time (BST) Cooler

Highball

Cucumber spear and mint

Muddler   **Bar spoon**

mint	6 leaves
gin	45 ml (1½ oz)
freshly pressed apple juice	30 ml (1 oz)
elderflower cordial	7½ ml (¼ oz)
soda water	to top up

Gently muddle the mint in a chilled glass and then three quarters-fill with crushed ice. Add the gin, apple juice and elderflower cordial and stir to combine. Top up with soda, stir once more and add more crushed ice.

Gin-focused Cocktails

Lemon Verbena Cooler

Highball

GARNISH

Lemon verbena

EQUIPMENT

Muddler   **Bar spoon**

lemon verbena leaves	8–10
lime, cut into wedges	¾
Simple Syrup (see page 58)	15 ml (½ oz)
gin (ideally a new wave gin with cucumber notes, like Hendrick's)	60 ml (2 oz)
soda water	to top up

Add the verbena leaves, lime and simple syrup to a chilled glass and muddle. Pour in the gin. Three-quarters fill the glass with crushed ice, churn with a bar spoon and top up with soda. Stir once, then garnish with a sprig of lemon verbena.

TIP
For a bigger verbena kick, you can make a verbena syrup by adding a small handful of lemon verbena leaves to the pan when you make the simple syrup recipe. Strain before storing.

The Green Vesper

gin	60 ml (2 oz)
vodka	30 ml (1 oz)
absinthe	15 ml (½ oz)

Combine all of the ingredients together in a Boston glass or shaker filled with ice. Stir to chill. Strain into a chilled glass. Twist lime zest over the drink and drop it in.

TIP

To make this even greener, you can add 15 ml (½ oz) rocket (arugula) syrup. To make it, just purée together simple syrup (see page 58) and a large handful of rocket (arugula) in a blender. Strain into a sterilised bottle (see page 55) using a muslin (cheesecloth) or coffee filter.

GLASSWARE

Coupe

GARNISH

Lime twist

EQUIPMENT

Shaker

Strainer

Coconut G & T

Highball

Mint sprig

Dried coconut shards

Muddler **Bar spoon**

lime	¼
mint leaves	2
gin	60 ml (2 oz)
coconut water	60 ml (2 oz)
tonic water	60 ml (2 oz)

Muddle the lime and mint together in a chilled glass and fill with cubed ice. Add the gin, coconut and tonic waters. Stir gently to combine and garnish with a sprig of mint and dried coconut shards.

TIP
Easy to turn into a batch cocktail – just times by four or eight.

Beach House

gin	60 ml (2 oz)
freshly squeezed lime juice	15 ml (½ oz)
coconut water	to top up

Pour the gin and lime juice into a chilled glass over crushed ice, top with coconut water and add a swizzle stick and lime slice to garnish.

TIP
Best served wearing a coconut-shell bikini.

GLASSWARE

Highball

GARNISH

Lime slice

EQUIPMENT

Swizzle stick

Smashed Cucumber

cucumber chunks	a handful
dill	1 sprig
freshly squeezed lime juice	15 ml (½ oz)
Simple Syrup (see page 58)	a dash
gin	60 ml (2 oz)
cucumber juice	30 ml (1 oz)
soda water	to top up

In a chilled glass, gently muddle a handful of cucumber chunks and the dill with the lime juice and simple syrup. Add the gin, cucumber juice and ice and stir gently to combine. Top up with chilled soda water and garnish with a cucumber spear and dill fronds.

TIPS
Add a sprig of mint if you like your herbs extra pungent.

GLASSWARE

Collins

GARNISH

**Cucumber spear
and dill fronds**

EQUIPMENT

Muddler

Bar spoon

Pine Forest

Coupe

Pine tips

Shaker

gin	60 ml (2 oz)
almond milk	60 ml (2 oz)
Pine Tip Syrup (see page 60)	30 ml (½ oz)

Shake the ingredients over ice, pour into a chilled glass and serve with 2–3 freshly picked pine tips to garnish.

White Lady

gin	60 ml (2 oz)
Cointreau or orange liqueur	15 ml (½ oz)
lemon juice, freshly squeezed	15 ml (½ oz)

Shake over ice and serve in a chilled glass. Simple.

TIP
Add a drop of orange blossom water to dial up the aroma.

Grapefruit & Tarragon Collins

Collins

Tarragon and grapefruit peel

Muddler

Shaker   **Strainer**

tarragon	3–4 blades
light brown sugar	1 tsp
gin	60 ml (2 oz)
pink or ruby grapefruit juice	60 ml (2 oz)
tonic water	to top up

Muddle the fresh tarragon and sugar in a shaker. Add a handful of ice cubes, the gin and grapefruit juice and shake, then strain into a chilled glass full of ice. Top up with chilled tonic water. Add a few blades of tarragon and grapefruit peel to garnish (see page 95).

TIP
Make sure your grapefruit juice is bought freshly squeezed or squeeze it at home with a juicer (hand-held or machine).

Gin-focused Cocktails

The Queen Mum

Tumbler or coupe

Orange peel

Mixing glass

Strainer

gin	60 ml (2 oz)
Dubonnet	60 ml (2 oz)
orange blossom water	a dash
Angostura bitters	a dash

Add the wet ingredients to a mixing glass and stir with ice, then strain into chilled glass with a rock of ice. Garnish with a large piece of orange peel.

TIP
Best served wearing a diamond tiara.

Arizona Cooler

gin	45 ml (1½ oz)
cranberry juice	60 ml (2 oz)
grapefruit juice	60 ml (2 oz)

Fill a chilled glass with ice, then pour in the gin followed by the cranberry and grapefruit juices. To garnish, squeeze a lime wedge over the top and drop into the drink.

TIP
Peyote, optional.

GLASSWARE

Collins

GARNISH

Lime wedge

Sloe Gin Cooler

Sloe Gin (see page 54)	60 ml (2 oz)
freshly squeezed lemon juice	22½ ml (¾ oz)
Simple Syrup (see page 58)	15 ml (½ oz)
soda water	to top up

Combine the gin, lemon juice and simple syrup in a shaker filled with ice. Shake hard to combine and chill. Strain into a chilled glass filled with fresh ice and top up with soda water. Garnish with a dehydrated orange slice.

GLASSWARE

Collins

GARNISH

Dehydrated orange slice

EQUIPMENT

Shaker   Strainer

Sloe Gin & Tempranillo Negroni

Sloe & Star Anise Gin (see page 54)	30 ml (1 oz)
Tempranillo Reduction (see page 57)	30 ml (1 oz)
Campari	60 ml (2 oz)

Stir the ingredients in a mixing glass over ice. Strain into a chilled glass filled with ice cubes. Garnish with the orange peel. See photo opposite.

GLASSWARE

Tumbler

GARNISH

Orange peel

EQUIPMENT

Mixing   Strainer
glass

The Rudolph

Coupe or martini

String of fresh redcurrants

gin	60 ml (2 oz)
St-Germain	30 ml (1 oz)
Champagne	to top up

Pour the gin and St-Germain into a chilled glass, top up with Champagne and garnish with a string of fresh redcurrants.

TIP
Make sure you chill the glass for extra festive frostiness.

Alaskan Thunder

gin	60 ml (2 oz)
yellow Chartreuse	22½ ml (¾ oz)
orange bitters	2 dashes

Combine all of the ingredients in a Boston glass or shaker filled with ice. Stir to combine and chill, then strain into a chilled glass. Zest a lemon rind over the drink and drop in with a cherry.

TIPS
To zest a lemon rind, simply cut a wide piece of lemon peel and twist it over the drink to release the oils.

GLASSWARE

Martini

GARNISH

Zested lemon rind

Cherry

EQUIPMENT

Boston Glass or shaker

Bar spoon

The Colby

Tumbler or coupe or martini

Fresh cranberries

Shaker   **Strainer**

gin	60 ml (2 oz)
St-Germain	30 ml (1 oz)
freshly squeezed lemon juice	15 ml (½ oz)
cranberry juice	90 ml (3 oz)
orange bitters	a dash

Shake the wet ingredients over ice, strain into a chilled glass, tumbler or coupe and garnish with fresh cranberries.

TIP
Who has fresh cranberries, except at Christmas? FYI it's fine to use frozen.

New Fashioned

really excellent gin	60 ml (2 oz)
Simple Syrup (see page 58)	a splash
Angostura bitters	a dash
orange bitters	a dash

Add the gin and syrup to a chilled heavy-based glass over a large piece of ice. Splash the bitters on top and garnish with a large strip of lime peel to bash against the drinker's nose.

GLASSWARE

Tumbler

GARNISH

Large strip of lime peel

Long Beach Iced Tea

gin	15 ml (½ oz)
vodka	15 ml (½ oz)
gold rum	15 ml (½ oz)
triple sec	15 ml (½ oz)
shop-bought sweet and sour mix	60 ml (2 oz)
cranberry juice	to top up

Add the gin, vodka, rum, triple sec and sweet and sour mix into a cocktail shaker filled with ice. Shake hard to combine, then strain into a chilled glass filled with fresh ice. Top up with cranberry juice and stir. Add lime wheels and mint sprigs to garnish.

GLASSWARE

Collins

GARNISH

Lime wheels and
mint sprigs

EQUIPMENT

Shaker   Strainer

Nice Pear

freshly squeezed pear juice	60 ml (2 oz)
premium gin	60 ml (2 oz)
Spiced Brown Sugar Syrup (see page 59)	15 ml (½ oz)

Shake the wet ingredients over ice, then strain into a chilled glass. Grate over a little crystallised ginger and add a sprig of mint to garnish. See photo opposite.

TIPS
Add a dash of fresh lime juice if your pear is a little too sweet.

GLASSWARE

Coupe

GARNISH

Grated crystallised ginger,
mint sprig and pear

EQUIPMENT

Shaker   Strainer

SOURS

& FIZZES

Lip-smacking, thirst-quenching sour-edged gin drinks and their soft, marshmallow-like foamy counterparts.

Red Wine Gin Sour

Pina Colada

Orange twist

Shaker   **Strainer**

gin	45 ml (1½ oz)
elderflower liqueur	22½ ml (¾ oz)
Simple Syrup (page 58)	15 ml (½ oz)
freshly squeezed lemon juice	15 ml (½ oz)
egg white	1
red wine	22½ ml (¾ oz)
orange bitters	a dash

Add the gin, elderflower, simple syrup, lemon juice and egg white to a cocktail shaker, dry shake by shaking vigorously without ice, then add ice and shake again until chilled. Strain into a chilled glass filled with ice and top with the red wine and a dash of bitters. Garnish with an orange twist (see page 95).

Sours & Fizzes

Gin Sour

Coupe

Candied lemon twist

Shaker   **Strainer**

gin	45 ml (1½ oz)
Aperol	15 ml (½ oz)
freshly squeezed lemon juice	30 ml (1 oz)
egg white	1
orange bitters	2 dashes

Add all of the ingredients, except the bitters, to a cocktail shaker filled with ice. Shake vigorously, then strain into a chilled glass. Garnish with 2 dashes of bitters and a candied lemon twist (see page 95).

TIP
Make candied lemon twists by dipping lemon twists in frothed egg whites, coating in sugar and leaving to dry overnight.

Cherry French 75

ripe, stoned cherries	a small handful
Cherry Heering liqueur	15 ml (½ oz)
freshly squeezed lemon juice	15 ml (½ oz)
rosewater	a dash
gin	60 ml (2 oz)
prosecco	to top up

Gently muddle the cherries, Cherry Heering, lemon juice and rosewater in a shaker. Add the gin and shake over ice. Strain into a chilled glass and top up with chilled prosecco. Garnish with a single cherry.

TIP
Swap out the Cherry Heering for a dash of Simple Syrup (see page 58).

GLASSWARE

Coupe or martini

GARNISH

Cherry

EQUIPMENT

Muddler

Shaker   **Strainer**

Rhubarb Sour

Coupe

Orange or lime peel

Shaker   **Strainer**

gin	60 ml (2 oz)
triple sec	30 ml (1 oz)
freshly squeezed lemon juice	30 ml (1 oz)
Rhubarb Syrup (see page 58)	120 ml (4 oz)
egg white	1

Shake the gin, triple sec, lemon juice, rhubarb syrup and egg white vigorously over ice. Strain into a chilled glass and garnish with orange or lime peel.

TIPS
Add star anise to your home-made Rhubarb Syrup for a little liquorice upgrade.

Sours & Fizzes

Gin Rickey

Highball

Lime wedge

Bar spoon

gin	60 ml (2 oz)
freshly squeezed lime juice	15 ml (½ oz)
Simple Syrup (see page 58)	15 ml (½ oz)
soda water	to top up

Pour the gin, lime juice and syrup into a chilled glass filled with ice cubes. Stir, then top up with soda water and garnish with a lime wedge. Serve with a straw.

Cucumber Mint Gin Fizz

mint sprig	1
cucumber, cut into spears	1
gin	60 ml (2 oz)
freshly squeezed lemon juice	a dash
tonic water	to top up

Bruise the mint sprig using a muddler, and add to the jug with most of the cucumber spears. Cover with the gin and chill for 2 hours in the fridge. Fill a chilled glass with a few ice cubes, add a fresh cucumber spear and the lemon juice and strain the chilled, infused gin into the glass. Top up with chilled tonic water.

GLASSWARE

Highball or tumbler

EQUIPMENT

Muddler

Jug   **Strainer**

Cherry Thyme Sour

GLASSWARE

Coupe

GARNISH

Thyme sprig

EQUIPMENT

Shaker

Strainer

gin	60 ml (2 oz)
triple sec	30 ml (1 oz)
freshly squeezed lime juice	30 ml (1 oz)
Cherry & Thyme Syrup (see page 60)	120 ml (4 oz)
egg white	1
Angostura bitters	a dash

Shake the gin, triple sec, lime juice, syrup and egg white vigorously over ice. Strain into a chilled glass, add a couple of drops of Angostura bitters and garnish with a sprig of thyme.

TIP
Make sure your home-made syrup uses dark, rich, soft cherries and fresh thyme for extra flavour. Drop a couple into each glass for extra cherry popping.

Spiced Rhubarb & Rose Ramos Gin Fizz

Coupe

Shaker

Strainer

gin	60 ml (2 oz)
Rhubarb, Ginger & Star Anise Syrup (see page 54)	60 ml (2 oz)
single (light) cream	30 ml (1 oz)
freshly squeezed lime juice	15 ml (½ oz)
freshly squeezed lemon juice	15 ml (½ oz)
egg white	1
rosewater	a dash
soda water	to top up

Shake the wet ingredients – except the soda water – for 30 seconds, then add ice and shake for another 30 seconds. Strain into a chilled glass and top up with soda water.

TIP
Add a couple of drops of Angostura bitters for extra punch.

Cucumber Rose Fizz

gin (ideally a grape-based gin or a new wave gin)	45 ml (1½ oz)
freshly squeezed lemon juice	22½ ml (¾ oz)
Lavender & Rose Syrup (see page 55)	15 ml (½ oz)
cucumber soda	60 ml (2 oz)

Three-quarters-fill a chilled glass with crushed ice. Add the gin, lemon juice and rose syrup and churn gently. Top up with cucumber soda. Churn once more and garnish with cucumber slices.

see page 55

GLASSWARE

Collins

GARNISH

Cucumber slices

EQUIPMENT

Bar spoon

New Orleans Fizz

(aka Ramos)

Pina Colada

Orange twist

Shaker

gin (ideally a London Gin or Old Tom)	45 ml (1½ oz)
freshly squeezed lime juice	15 ml (½ oz)
freshly squeezed lemon juice	15 ml (½ oz)
Simple Syrup (see page 58)	30 ml (1 oz)
single (light) cream	60 ml (2 oz)
orange blossom water	2 dashes
vanilla essence	3 drops
egg white	1
soda water	to top up
orange bitters	a dash

Combine all of the ingredients, except the soda water and orange bitters, in a cocktail shaker. Dry shake the drink without ice and then add ice and shake again. Pour into a chilled glass and top up with soda water. Garnish with a dash of orange bitters and an orange twist (see page 95).

Gooseberry Gin Fizz

fresh gooseberries	a handful
light brown sugar	1 tbsp
gin	60 ml (2 oz)
elderflower cordial	30 ml (1 oz)
freshly squeezed lime juice	15 ml (½ oz)
cloudy sparkling lemonade	to top up

Muddle the gooseberries and sugar together in a shaker, then add the gin, elderflower cordial and lime juice and shake. Strain into a chilled glass full of ice and top up with lemonade. Garnish with fresh, sliced gooseberries.

GLASSWARE

Highball

GARNISH

Fresh sliced gooseberries

EQUIPMENT

Muddler

Shaker   **Strainer**

Gilbert Grape

Highball

Thyme sprig

Muddler

Shaker   **Strainer**

green seedless grapes	a handful
thyme sprigs	2–3
light brown sugar	1 tbsp
gin	60 ml (2 oz)
Spiced Brown Sugar Syrup (see page 59)	30 ml (1 oz)
freshly squeezed lime juice	15 ml (½ oz)
soda water	to top up

Roast the grapes whole until soft and caramelised (see page 209). Allow to cool, then muddle them with the thyme and sugar in a shaker. Add the gin, sugar syrup and lime juice and shake. Strain into a chilled glass full of ice and top up with soda water. Garnish with more fresh thyme sprigs.

Borage Citrus Fizz

gin	45 ml (1½ oz)
freshly squeezed lemon juice	30 ml (1 oz)
orange bitters	a dash
Borage Syrup (see page 59)	30 ml (1 oz)
soda water	to top up

Three-quarters-fill a chilled glass with crushed ice. Add the gin, lemon juice, bitters and borage syrup and stir to mix. Top up with soda water. Stir very gently, then add a borage flower and lemon twist to garnish (see page 95).

GLASSWARE

Jam jar

GARNISH

Borage flower

Lemon twist

EQUIPMENT

Bar spoon

Sour Cherry Sling

gin	45 ml (1½ oz)
Cointreau or orange liqueur	22½ ml (¾ oz)
freshly squeezed lime juice	15 ml (½ oz)
cherry purée	22½ ml (¾ oz)
sour cherry bitters	2 dashes
soda water	to top up

Three-quarters-fill a chilled glass with crushed ice. Add the gin, Cointreau, lime juice, purée and bitters. Stir to combine, top up with soda water and then carefully stir again. Squeeze the lime wedge over the drink and drop it in with a cherry.

Jam jar

Lime wedge

Cherry

Bar spoon

Rhubarb Collins

Highball

Curl of rhubarb

Muddler

Bar spoon

mint leaves	4–6
gin	45 ml (1½ oz)
Rhubarb, Ginger & Star Anise Syrup (see page 58)	30 ml (1 oz)
freshly squeezed lemon juice	22½ ml (¾ oz)
orange bitters	a dash
soda water	to top up

Gently muddle mint leaves in the bottom of a chilled glass. Add the gin, rhubarb syrup, lemon juice and bitters. Stir, then three-quarters-fill with crushed ice. Stir the drink, top up with soda water and stir gently once more. Cap off the drink with more crushed ice and garnish with a curl of rhubarb.

TIPS
To make rhubarb curls, first use a vegetable peeler to make thin slices of rhubarb. Soak the slices in simple syrup for 5 minutes and then put into a 110°C (225°F/Gas ½) oven for about an hour until the liquid has evaporated. Curl the warm strips around a wooden spoon handle to make spirals and leave to cool for about 10 minutes.

French 77

gin	30 ml (1 oz)
elderflower liqueur	15 ml (½ oz)
freshly squeezed lemon juice	15 ml (½ oz)
orange bitters	a dash
Champagne	to top up

Place the gin, elderflower liqueur, freshly squeezed lemon juice and bitters into a cocktail shaker filled with ice. Shake hard to chill. Strain into a chilled coupe glass and top up with Champagne. Garnish with a lemon twist (see page 95).

TIPS
Prosecco or cava work equally well if your Champagne cellar is empty.

GLASSWARE

Coupe

GARNISH

Lemon twist

EQUIPMENT

Shaker

Violet Fizz

gin	37½ ml (1¼ oz)
crème de violette	15 ml (½ oz)
freshly squeezed lemon juice	7½ ml (¼ oz)
Simple Syrup (see page 58)	7½ ml (¼ oz)
soda water	to top up

Pour the gin, crème de violette, lemon juice and simple syrup into a cocktail shaker filled with ice. Shake well, then strain into a chilled glass. Top up with soda water, stir and serve with sweets on the side.

TIP
You can add a tablespoon of egg white if you want a frothier drink.

GLASSWARE

Champagne

GARNISH

Pack of parma violets

EQUIPMENT

Shaker

Strainer   Bar spoon

BRUNCH

DRINKS

Lip-smacking, thirst-quenching sour-edged gin drinks and their soft, marshmallow-like foamy counterparts.

Pink Gin Spritz

Champagne

Shaker

gin	60 ml (2 oz)
Aperol	30 ml (1 oz)
Campari	15 ml (½ oz)
Spiced Brown Sugar Syrup (see page 59)	a dash
pink grapefruit juice	to top up

Shake the gin, Aperol, Campari and brown sugar syrup over ice. Add to a chilled glass and top with the chilled pink grapefruit juice.

TIP
Make sure your grapefruit juice is ice-cold.

Brunch Drinks

Southside Royale

Coupe

Crystallised mint leaf

Shaker

Strainer

lime, cut into wedges	½
mint sprigs	2 (8–10 leaves)
Simple Syrup (see page 58)	15 ml (½ oz)
gin	60 ml (2 oz)
Champagne	to top up

Muddle the lime wedges, mint and simple syrup in a cocktail shaker. Add the gin and fill with ice. Shake hard to chill and then double strain into a chilled glass. Top with Champagne and a crystallised mint leaf.

TIPS

You can buy crystallised mint sprigs or make your own by dipping mint leaves in egg white and sugar and leaving to air-dry overnight.

Bees Knees

gin	60 ml (2 oz)
freshly squeezed lemon juice	22½ ml (¾ oz)
raw honey	22½ ml (¾ oz)
orange bitters	a dash
freshly squeezed orange juice (optional)	15 ml (½ oz)

Place all of the ingredients into a cocktail shaker filled with ice. Shake hard to combine, then strain into a chilled glass. Top with a candied lemon twist (see pages 95 and 136).

GLASSWARE

Coupe

GARNISH

Candied lemon twist

EQUIPMENT

Shaker

Strainer

Naked Peach

Coupe

Peach slices and rosemary

Blender

Sieve **Strainer**

large roasted or very ripe peach	1
light brown sugar	1 tsp
freshly squeezed lime juice	15 ml (½ oz)
gin	60 ml (2 oz)
lime zest	a pinch
Rosemary-infused Syrup (see page 163)	15 ml (½ oz)
lemonade	to top up

Purée the roasted peach, sugar and lime juice in a blender, then sieve. Shake the gin, peach purée, lime zest and syrup over ice in a cocktail shaker, then pour into the chilled glass. Top up with chilled lemonade and garnish with peach slices and rosemary.

TIP
Chop the peach in half and remove the stone. Roast until soft.

Brunch Drinks

Sloe Ginger

mint leaves	4
Sloe Gin (see page 54)	60 ml (2 oz)
pomegranate juice	60 ml (2 oz)
pomegranate seeds	approximately 6
ginger beer	to top up

Gently muddle the mint in the bottom of the glass. Three-quarters-fill with crushed ice, add the sloe gin, pomegranate juice and seeds and stir to combine. Top up with the ginger beer and stir gently. Top up with more crushed ice and garnish with a sprig of mint.

Sloe Gin (see page 54)

GLASSWARE

Tumbler or highball

GARNISH

Mint sprig

EQUIPMENT

Muddler   **Bar spoon**

Rosemary Gin Paloma

gin	60 ml (2 oz)
rosemary bitters	a dash
freshly squeezed lime juice	15 ml (½ oz)
Simple Syrup (see page 58) or Rosemary-infused Syrup (see tip)	15 ml (½ oz)
grapefruit soda	to top up

Combine the gin, rosemary bitters, lime juice and simple syrup in a cocktail shaker filled with ice. Shake vigorously, then strain into a chilled glass filled with ice. Top up with soda water, stir once and garnish with a sprig of rosemary and grapefruit slice.

TIP
To make the rosemary-infused syrup, just add a few sprigs of rosemary to the pan when you're making the simple syrup recipe. Strain before bottling and add a fresh sprig to the bottle.

GLASSWARE

Highball

GARNISH

Rosemary sprig and a grapefruit slice

EQUIPMENT

Shaker

Strainer   **Bar spoon**

Red Snapper

Collins

GARNISH

Sea salt rim, lime wedge and celery stick

EQUIPMENT

Saucer to salt

Bar spoon

gin	45 ml (1½ oz)
freshly squeezed lemon juice	7½ ml (¼ oz)
tomato juice	120 ml (4 oz)
hot sauce (ideally Frank's but others are good too)	a dash
Worcestershire sauce	2 dashes
hot horseradish	½ tsp
celery salt	a pinch
salt and black pepper	a pinch

For the salt rim, squish a lime wedge along the edge of a chilled glass and dip in sea salt, then fill the glass with ice. Add all of the ingredients and stir well using a long bar spoon. Squeeze a wedge of lime over the top and add the celery stick.

TIPS
Use Clamato juice instead of tomato juice for a Gin Caesar.

Green Snapper

freshly pressed pineapple juice	120 ml (4 oz)
freshly squeezed lime juice	15 ml (½ oz)
jalapeño chilli sauce	2 dashes
coriander (cilantro) leaves and mint	4 of each
salt	a pinch
gin	45 ml (1½ oz)

Place the pineapple juice, lime juice, chilli, herbs and salt into a blender and blend until smooth. Fill a chilled glass with ice, add the gin and top up with the blended juice. Stir and add your choice of garnish.

TIPS
You can also combine all of the ingredients in the blender with a scoop of crushed ice and blend to make a (not so healthy) smoothie.

GLASSWARE

Highball

GARNISH

Mint, coriander (cilantro) or a long slice of green chilli

EQUIPMENT

Blender

Bar spoon

Ginger Greyhound

GLASSWARE

Coupe or martini

GARNISH

Grated crystallised ginger

EQUIPMENT

Shaker

gin	60 ml (2 oz)
freshly squeezed grapefruit juice	100 ml (3½ oz)
Spiced Brown Sugar Syrup (see page 59)	a dash

Shake the wet ingredients in a cocktail shaker with ice cubes and vigour, then pour into a chilled glass. Top with 1 teaspoon grated crystallised ginger.

TIP
Rosy it up with pink grapefruit juice, because why not?

Brunch Drinks

Royal Orange Blossom

**Coupe or
Large Champagne flute**

GARNISH

Dehydrated orange slice

EQUIPMENT

Shaker

Strainer

gin	22½ ml (¾ oz)
mandarin vodka	7½ ml (¼ oz)
freshly squeezed orange juice	22½ ml (¾ oz)
Champagne	to top up

Pour the gin, vodka and orange juice into a cocktail shaker filled with ice. Shake hard to chill and mix the drink. Strain into a chilled glass and top up with Champagne. Garnish with a dehydrated orange slice.

TIP
It doesn't have to be Champagne – prosecco and cava also work.

Angel's Delight

gin	30 ml (1 oz)
Cointreau (or other triple sec)	30 ml (1 oz)
single (light) cream	45 ml (1½ oz)
grenadine	7½ ml (¼ oz)

Place all of the ingredients into a cocktail shaker. Dry shake by shaking without ice first and then adding ice and shaking again. Strain into a chilled glass and add a marshmallow to garnish.

TIP
Sweet and creamy and very pink, this also works with sloe gin. A great alternative to dessert.

GLASSWARE

Coupe

GARNISH

Marshmallows

EQUIPMENT

Shaker

Strainer

Gin & Jam Cocktail

gin	60 ml (2 oz)
freshly squeezed lemon juice	30 ml (1 oz)
raspberry jam	2 tsp
Simple Syrup (see page 58)	15 ml (½ oz)

Shake the gin, lemon juice, 1 teaspoon of jam and simple syrup over ice. Strain into a chilled glass filled with crushed ice, stir in the second teaspoon of jam and garnish with a mint sprig. Cut out the simple syrup if you don't have a sweet tooth. See photo opposite.

TIP
Use any gourmet dark berry jam – or even marmalade, if you're feeling it.

Highball or Tumbler

GARNISH

Mint sprig

EQUIPMENT

Shaker **Strainer**

Gin Power Shot

Coupe

Ginger slice

Juicer (machine)

Shaker   **Strainer**

freshly squeezed ginger juice	15 ml (½ oz)
gin	60 ml (2 oz)
cloudy apple juice	30 ml (1 oz)
freshly squeezed lime juice	15 ml (½ oz)
Simple Syrup (see page 58)	a dash

Juice a thumb-sized piece of fresh ginger and add to a shaker with the remaining wet ingredients. Shake over ice. Add more simple syrup, to taste. Strain into a chilled glass and garnish with a slice of fresh ginger.

TIP
Fresh apple juice (the cloudy kind) works best.

Lillet Rose

Lillet Rose vermouth	45 ml (1½ oz)
gin (ideally a grape-based gin or a new wave gin)	45 ml (1½ oz)
red grapefruit juice	30 ml (1 oz)
freshly squeezed lemon juice	15 ml (½ oz)
orange bitters	a dash

Combine all of the ingredients in a Boston glass or shaker filled with ice. Stir for 30 seconds to combine and chill. Strain into a chilled glass and garnish with edible flower petals.

GLASSWARE

Coupe

GARNISH

Edible flower petals

EQUIPMENT

Boston glass or shaker

Bar spoon   **Strainer**

GLASSWARE

Martini

GARNISH

Orange twist

EQUIPMENT

Shaker   **Strainer**

Fine mesh strainer

Breakfast Martini

gin	60 ml (2 oz)
Grand Marnier	15 ml (½ oz)
freshly squeezed lemon juice	15 ml (½ oz)
Seville orange marmalade	1 tsp

Place all of the ingredients into a cocktail shaker filled with ice. Shake vigorously and then double strain into a chilled glass. See photo opposite.

TIP
Double straining is to place your strainer on the cocktail shaker as normal and then pour through a fine mesh strainer into the glass. A tea strainer works well.

GLASSWARE

Highball

GARNISH

Orange and lemon slices

EQUIPMENT

Bar spoon

Gin St Clements

gin (ideally a London Dry Gin)	30 ml (1 oz)
mandarin vodka	30 ml (1 oz)
freshly squeezed orange juice	30 ml (1 oz)
freshly squeezed lemon juice	30 ml (1 oz)
tonic water	to top up

Half-fill a chilled glass with ice, add all of the ingredients except the tonic and stir to combine. Top up with tonic and stir gently. Garnish with a slice of orange and lemon.

TIP
This is a classic with the added punch of the mandarin vodka.

Brunch Drinks

Cucumber Lemonade

Highball

Cucumber spear

Shaker

Strainer

gin	60 ml (2 oz)
freshly squeezed cucumber juice	30 ml (1 oz)
freshly squeezed lemon juice	15 ml (½ oz)
Simple Syrup (see page 58) or agave syrup	a dash
chilled soda water	to top up

Shake the gin, cucumber and lemon juices and syrup over ice. Add a cucumber spear and ice cubes to a chilled glass, strain the drink and pour into the glass. Top up with soda water.

TIP
Garnish with a sprig of mint.

Blood Orange Gin & Tonic

gin	60 ml (2 oz)
freshly squeezed blood orange juice	60 ml (2 oz)
freshly squeezed lime juice	a dash
premium tonic water	to top up

Shake the gin, blood orange juice and lime juice over ice. Strain into a chilled glass filled with ice and top with chilled premium tonic water. Garnish with orange peel.

GLASSWARE

Highball

GARNISH

Orange peel

EQUIPMENT

Shaker

Strainer

Watermelon G & T

Highball

Small wedge of watermelon

Mint sprig

Shaker   **Strainer**

gin	60 ml (2 oz)
freshly squeezed watermelon juice	60 ml (2 oz)
freshly squeezed lemon juice	a dash
premium elderflower tonic water	to top up

Shake the gin, watermelon juice and lemon juice over ice. Strain into a chilled glass filled with ice and top up with tonic water. Garnish with a small wedge of watermelon and a mint sprig. Serve with a straw.

TIP
Supersize it into a punch with chunks of watermelon and slices of citrus.

Brunch Drinks

BATCH COCKTA

LS & PUNCHES

Throwing yourself a shindig? Discover the perfect batch recipes and punches to make gin the centre of backyard BBQs, buck's nights, and bar/bat mitzvahs.

Orange and lime slices and pineapple chunks or slices

Pitcher and glasses

Freezerproof container

Blender

Pitcher and glasses

The Snoop
(aka Gin & Juice)

freshly squeezed lime juice	175 ml (6 oz)
Cinnamon Syrup (see page 61)	175 ml (6 oz)
gin	750 ml (25 oz)
cranberry juice	350 ml (12 oz)
pineapple juice	350 ml (12 oz)
freshly squeezed orange juice	350 ml (12 oz)

Add the lime juice, cinnamon syrup and gin to the pitcher and stir well. Add the remaining wet ingredients over large ice cubes. Serve in paper cups and garnish with the slices of fruit. See photo opposite.

TIPS
Go heavy on the citrus – you want it sharp enough to knock your dentures out.

Frozen G & T

gin	180 ml (6 oz)
freshly squeezed lime juice	60 ml (2 oz)
concentrated tonic syrup (the sort you use for a SodaStream and available at most supermarkets)	60 ml (2 oz)
your favourite bitters (optional)	3 dashes

Combine all of the ingredients (except the ice) in a large freezerproof container. Place in the freezer for at least an hour. Remove the mix from the freezer, place in a blender with 4 scoops of crushed ice and blend until smooth. Served in chilled glasses and garnish with the lime wheels.

TIP
Putting the mix in the freezer first ensures your drinks stay slushy and cold.

Batch Cocktails & Punches

Honey Beer Punch

GLASSWARE

Highball

GARNISH

Lemon slice

EQUIPMENT

Mixing glass   **Bar spoon**

honey	1 tsp
hot water	a splash
freshly squeezed lemon juice	15 ml (½ oz)
gin	60 ml (2 oz)
premium beer	to top up

Melt a generous teaspoon of honey in a mixing glass with a splash of hot water and allow to cool. Add to a chilled glass filled with ice, lemon juice and gin. Stir and top with chilled beer, adding a lemon slice to garnish.

Honey Bear Gin Punch

gin	600 ml (21 oz)
honey	250 ml (8½oz) thinned with 1 tbsp water
freshly squeezed lemon juice	250 ml (8½ oz/1 cup)
Angostura bitters	a splash
prosecco	to top up

Mix the ingredients in a punch bowl (with an ice block) or pitcher (with ice) and add the sage sprigs and lemon slices. Serve over ice-filled glasses.

TIP
Swap the chilled prosecco for beer if you're not that posh.

SERVES 10–12

GLASSWARE

Punch glass

GARNISH

Sage sprigs and lemons slices

EQUIPMENT

Mixing glass   **Bar spoon**

Punch glass

Thin orange and lime slices

Punchbowl or pitcher

Aperol Gin Punch

gin	1.25 litres (2¼ pints)
Aperol	725 ml (1¼ pints)
Galliano	250 ml (8½ oz/1 cup)
freshly squeezed lime juice	500 ml (17 oz)
freshly squeezed pink grapefruit juice	625 ml (1 pint)
orange bitters	a splash
prosecco	to top up

Mix the ingredients in a punch bowl (with an ice block) or pitcher (with ice) and add the orange and lime slices. Serve over ice-filled glasses. See photo opposite.

Punch glass

Soft summer fruits and lime wheels

Bar spoon **Large pitcher**

Blackberry & Lavender Spritz

gin	600 ml (10 oz)
crème de cassis	120 ml (4 oz)
freshly squeezed lime juice	120 ml (4 oz)
blackberry purée	120 ml (4 oz)
Lavender & Rose Syrup (see page 57)	120 ml (4 oz)
prosecco	750 ml (25 oz)

Three-quarters-fill a pitcher with ice. Add the gin, crème de cassis, lime juice, blackberry purée and syrup. Add the summer fruits and lime wheels, then top up with a bottle of chilled prosecco and stir gently. Serve in chilled glasses.

Batch Cocktails & Punches

Summer Blueberry Cocktail

SERVES 8–10

GLASSWARE

Highball

GARNISH

Mint sprig and few whole blueberries

EQUIPMENT

Blender

gin	480 ml (16 oz)
vodka	240 ml (8 oz)
frozen blueberries	400 g (14 oz)
freshly squeezed lime juice	90 ml (3 oz)
Mint Syrup (see page 61)	45 ml (1½ oz)
mint leaves	20
sparkling mineral water	to top up

Whizz the gin, vodka, blueberries, lime juice, syrup and mint leaves in a blender, then add a little chilled mineral water to loosen the liquid. Pour into a chilled glass full of ice, garnish with a mint sprig, a few whole blueberries and serve with a straw.

TIPS
Add a little lemon juice if it's a bit too sweet. Simple Syrup (page 58) will work if you don't have mint.

French 75 Punch

SERVES 8–10

gin	480 ml (16 oz)
freshly squeezed lemon juice	240 ml (8 oz) – roughly 5 lemons
Simple Syrup (see page 58)	120 ml (4 oz)
orange bitters	6 dashes
Champagne or prosecco	750 ml (25 oz)

Add all of the ingredients together (except the Champagne) in a large jug and stir to combine. You can then refrigerate this mix ready for when needed. To serve, simply fill a punch bowl with ice and add your refrigerated mix. Pour the Champagne slowly over the top and stir gently. Serve in chilled glasses and garnish with the citrus slices.

TIP
For an extra kick, add a dash of absinthe.

GLASSWARE

Punch glass

GARNISH

Blood orange and lemon slices

EQUIPMENT

Jug

Bar spoon   **Large punch bowl**

Hot Gin Punch

Punch glass

Cinnamon sticks

Large saucepan

Strainer   **Heatproof punch bowl or a tea pot**

gin	600 ml (20 oz)
Madeira wine	600 ml (20 oz)
lemon zest	5 strips
orange wheels	5
pineapple slices	5
Simple Syrup (see page 58)	90 ml (3 oz)
freshly squeezed lemon juice	30 ml (1 oz)
freshly squeezed orange juice	30 ml (1 oz)
ground cinnamon	1 tsp
cloves	3
grated nutmeg	a pinch
brown sugar	1 tsp

Add all of the ingredients to a large saucepan and simmer for 20 minutes. Pour straight from the pan into your serving bowl or tea pot and serve in heat-resistent glasses with cinnamon sticks to garnish.

Batch Cocktails & Punches

MORNING AFTER

Steady your nerves or forget your indiscretions:
these are the gin-based remedies to give your
walk of shame a little spring in your step.

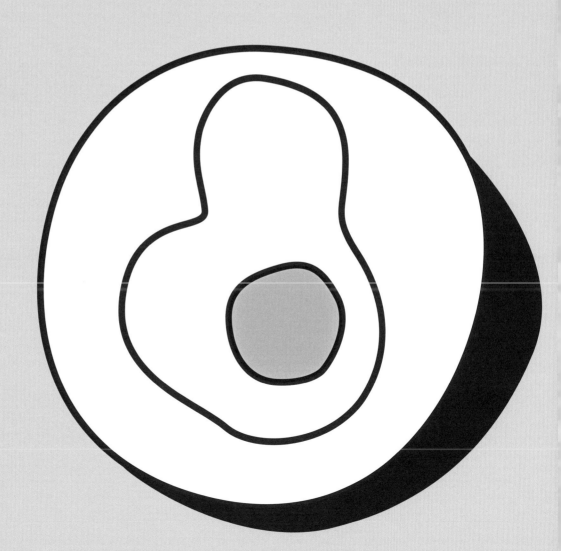

Corpse Reviver No. 2

Martini

Lemon twist

Boston glass or shaker

Bar spoon    **Strainer**

absinthe	a dash
gin	60 ml (2 oz)
Cointreau or orange liqueur	22½ ml (¾ oz)
freshly squeezed lemon juice	22½ ml (¾ oz)
dry vermouth	22½ ml (¾ oz)

Pour the absinthe into a chilled glass, swirl around to coat the inside and then discard. Add the rest of the ingredients to a Boston glass or shaker and stir with a long bar spoon to chill. Strain into the prepared glass and garnish with a lemon twist (see page 95).

The Morning After

Marmajito

lemon, cut into small chunks	¼
mint leaves	8–10
Seville orange marmalade	2 tsp
gin	45 ml (1½ oz)
Elderflower Syrup (see page 61)	15 ml (½ oz)
tonic water	to top up

Place the lemon, mint and marmalade into the bottom of a chilled glass and muddle. Three-quarters-fill with crushed ice and then add the gin and elderflower syrup and churn gently. Top up with tonic water and slide the dehydrated orange wheel down the edge of the glass.

GLASSWARE

Highball

GARNISH

Dehydrated orange wheel

EQUIPMENT

Muddler

Bar spoon

Silver Fizz

gin	60 ml (2 oz)
freshly squeezed lemon juice	22½ ml (¾ oz)
Simple Syrup (see page 58)	15 ml (½ ml)
egg white	1
soda water	to top up
orange bitters	a dash

Add the gin, lemon juice, simple syrup and egg white to a cocktail shaker filled with ice. Shake hard to chill. Strain into a chilled glass filled with ice and top up with soda. Dash the orange bitters on top of the foam to garnish.

TIP
You can use an egg yolk instead to make a Gold Fizz or add the yolk to a shot glass with salt and pepper as a chaser. What doesn't kill you...

GLASSWARE

Highball

EQUIPMENT

Shaker

Strainer

Totally Nuts!

gin	30 ml (1 oz)
Frangelico hazelnut liqueur	15 ml (½ oz)
amaretto almond liqueur	15 ml (½ oz)
mixed nuts	a small handful
vanilla ice cream	2 scoops
banana	¼

Place all of the ingredients into the blender with ½ scoop of crushed ice and blend until you have a lovely thick milkshake. Pour into a chilled glass and top with whipped cream and crushed amaretti biscuits. See photo opposite.

TIP
You can serve without alcohol – just use 60 ml (2 oz) almond milk instead.

**Orange twist and jaffa
cake (or other chocolate/
orange-based cake/biscuit
snack)**

EQUIPMENT

Turbo G & T

gin	30 ml (1 oz)
tonic water	120 ml (4 oz)
Kahlúa coffee liqueur	7½ ml (¼ oz)
cold brew coffee	15 ml (½ oz)

Fill a chilled glass with ice and add the gin and tonic water. Mix the Kahlúa with the cold brew coffee in a jug and then carefully pour over the drink so that it mixes slowly. Garnish with an orange twist (see page 95) serve with a jaffa cake.

TIP
You can buy ready-made cold brew coffee or make your own overnight. If you're in a hurry, just cheat and use a cooled shot of espresso for a more rough-and-ready drink.

The Morning After

G & T Pancakes with Lemon Syrup

EQUIPMENT

Small pan

Sieve

Mixing bowl

Non-stick frying pan

BATTER	
self-raising flour	200 g (7 oz/1½ cups)
cream of tartar	1 tsp
milk	60 ml (2 oz)
gin	60 ml (2 oz)
tonic water	200 ml (7 oz)
non-stick cooking spray	
SYRUP	
water	240 ml (8 oz/1 cup)
caster (superfine) sugar	240 g (8½ oz/generous 1 cup)
freshly squeezed lemon juice	300 ml (9½ oz/1¼ cups)

To make the syrup — combine the water and sugar in a small pan and gently bring to the boil. Remove from the heat, cool for 15 minutes, then add the lemon juice.

To make the pancakes — sift the self-raising flour and cream of tartar into a bowl. Make a well in the middle of the flour and add the rest of the wet ingredients, stirring gently to combine. Leave to rest in the fridge for 10 minutes.

Heat a non-stick frying pan and spray with non-stick cooking spray. Drop in 2–3 tablespoons of batter and cook the pancakes for 1–2 minutes on each side, or until golden. Serve the pancakes stacked up and drizzle with the lemon syrup.

The Ultimate Hangover Bacon Roll

dried juniper berries	3–4
full-fat cream cheese	125 g (4½ oz/½ cup)
honey	1 tbsp
tomato ketchup	6 tbsp
smoked streaky bacon	6 slices
eggs	2
brioche rolls	2
salt and black pepper	
hot sauce	to serve

Grind the juniper berries in a pestle and mortar, then whisk into the cream cheese.

Mix the honey and ketchup together.

Place the bacon in a dry non-stick frying pan and cook over a medium-high heat until crisp. Set the bacon to one side.

Using the same frying pan, quickly fry the eggs in the leftover bacon fat.

Slice the brioche in half and spread cream cheese on the base. Add the bacon and egg to the roll, season with salt and pepper and top with the ketchup and a dash or two of hot sauce.

EQUIPMENT

Pestle and mortar

Mixing bowl

Non-stick frying pan

Unbelievably easy
serve-at-home toasted snacks,
dips, and treats with a retro edge.

BAR

Cocktail sticks

Cheese & Pineapple

The kid's party essential; serve in a malformed edible hedgehog shape for extra authenticity.

Serves: 6–8

Gruyère cheese	200 g (7 oz)
fresh pineapple	200 g (7 oz)
black pepper	

Cut the Gruyère into 2 cm (¾ in) cubes. Carve the pineapple, cutting away the pits. Chop into slices, remove the core and cut into 2 cm (¾ in) cubes. Season with a pinch of freshly ground black pepper and spear both with a cocktail stick (toothpick).

Serve the spears rammed into a melon or grapefruit half, et voila! Allow for 3–4 per person.

Equipment

Cocktail sticks (toothpicks)

Halloumi, Harrisa & Naan Bread

These spicy little numbers have the squeaky, salty tang of the halloumi with the mild heat of the harissa.

Serves: 4

naan breads	2
block of halloumi	200 g (7 oz)
olive oil	a splash
lemon wedge	
harissa used	1 tbsp
cucumber raita and mango chutney	to serve (optional)

Bake the naan breads in a 107°C (325°F/Gas 3) oven until just turning crisp (yet still soft in the middle). Cut the halloumi into thin slices and fry in the oil in a non-stick frying pan until golden. Season with a squeeze of lemon.

Spread harissa on the naan and add a piece of halloumi, then slice the bread and cheese into 2–3 cm (1 in) square slices. Build up on a cocktail stick (toothpick) starting with the naan bread, then the halloumi, then top with another square of naan. Serve with cucumber raita and mango chutney.

Equipment

Non-stick frying pan, cocktail sticks (toothpicks)

Hot Dips

Artichoke Dip

Hot mayonnaise? Yes, it may be a food crime, but it's unforgettably tasty: served here as one of the essential components of the artichoke dip.

Serves: 4

garlic cloves, finely chopped	3
artichoke hearts in brine, drained and roughly chopped	3 tins
Parmesan, finely grated	300 g (10½ oz)
hot cayenne pepper	1 heaped tsp
mayonnaise	220 g (8 oz/1 cup)
breadcrumbs	a handful
toasted baguette slices or crudités	to serve

Mix together the garlic and the artichoke hearts, then add the Parmesan and cayenne and stir in the mayonnaise (add a little more mayo if the mixture seems too dry). Add the gloopy mixture to a small ovenproof dish and bake in a 180°C (356°F/Gas 4) oven for 20 minutes or until golden and bubbling. Sprinkle with breadcrumbs for the final few minutes. Serve hot with toasted baguette slices or crudités.

Equipment

Ovenproof dish

Hot Camembert & Salsa Verde

Serve anyone a whole hot, wobbling, stinky cheese and they'll love you forever. Fact.

Serves: 6

wooden boxed whole camembert cheese	1
garlic cloves, 2 cut into chunky slices	4
coriander (cilantro)	a small bunch
flat-leaf parsley	a small bunch
green jalapeño chilli	1
1 large lime	juice of
spring onions (scallions)	4–5
cornichons	3–4
olive oil	2–3 tbsp
salt and black pepper	
toasts or crudités	to serve

Unbox and unwrap the camembert, ram in the garlic and replace the camembert into its box. Place on a baking tray and bake in a 180°C (356°F/Gas 4) oven for 10–15 minutes or until the surface wobbles to the touch. Finely chop the coriander stalks and blend with the remaining garlic and other ingredients. Spoon onto the hot camembert and serve with toasts or crudités to dip.

Equipment

Baking tray, blender

Chilled Dips

Smoked Mackerel & Horseradish

This delicious, fishy dip has a fiery little horseradish kick. Best served with griddle-toasted sourdough.

Serves: 6

smoked mackerel, skin removed	1
hot horseradish cream	1 tbsp
soft cream cheese	180 g (6½ oz/¾ cup)
low-fat crème fraîche	2 tbsp
juice and zest of	1 lemon
flat-leaf parsley	a small bunch
chives	a small bunch
olive oil	a splash
salt and pepper	
toasts, crackers or crudités	to serve

Blend all the ingredients to a slightly lumpy (yet delicious) consistency, and serve with toasts, crackers or crudités.

Equipment

Blender

Baba Ganoush

The famous Levantine dish of gloopy, mashed roasted aubergine with a smoky, spiced edge. Curious-looking, yet delicious.

Serves: 4

large aubergines (eggplants), roasted or grilled	3
garlic cloves, crushed with salt	3
extra virgin olive oil	3 tbsp
tahini	2 tbsp
flat-leaf parsley, roughly chopped	Small bunch of
juice of	1 lemon
salt and black pepper	
smoked paprika, to garnish	1 tsp

Roast aubergines (eggplants) in a 200°C (400°F/Gas 6) oven for about 30 minutes until soft, then leave to cool for 15 minutes. Scoop out the soft, roasted aubergine flesh and squish (rather than blend) with the other ingredients. Serve with a sprinkling of smoked paprika on top.

Apocalypse Salsa

Get dipping like it's the end of the world with this sweet, fruity and fiery salsa.

Serves: 6

fresh pineapple, peeled and cored	½
coriander (cilantro)	a bunch of
green jalapeño chilli	1
spring onions (scallions)	4–5
yellow tomatoes	2
juice of limes	2
zest of lime	1
red onion	1
dried chilli flakes	1 tsp
salt and black pepper	

Cut the pineapple into small 5 mm (¼ in) chunks and set a third aside. Finely chop the coriander stalks and blend with the pineapple, jalapeño, spring onions, coriander stalks and leaves, tomatoes, lime juice and zest, red onion and dried chilli flakes to a lumpy consistency. Stir in the remaining pineapple chunks, season to taste and serve.

Bruschetta & Toasts

Dirty Toasted Cheese

You like your snacks dirty? Then toasted cheese is your ultimate dish. Serve with a sticky squeezy bottle of BBQ sauce for extra filthiness.

Serves: 1–2

butter	1 tbsp
sage leaves	10–12
garlic cloves, roughly chopped	2
large slices of good-quality white bread	2
Dijon mustard	1 tsp
mature Cheddar cheese slices	
small cornichons, to serve	

Melt the butter with the sage leaves and garlic and fry in a non-stick frying pan on a low-medium heat briefly. Dip the bread slices in so both sides soak up a little butter, then remove one slice for a moment, smear on the mustard, add the cheese slices and top off with the remaining slice of bread. Add the odd scrap of cheese to the pan. Weigh down with a heavy, heatproof plate and cook for 2–3 minutes on a low heat until each side is golden and gooey with crispy cheese scraps. Cut into squares and serve immediately with a tumble of cornichons.

Equipment

Non-stick frying pan, heavy heatproof plate

Bruschetta

The classic Italian summer-powered snack. Use the best quality tomatoes you can buy/steal.

Serves: 4–6

juicy tomatoes, at room temperature	5
basil leaves	a bunch
garlic cloves, finely sliced	2
red wine vinegar	1 tbsp
extra virgin olive oil, plus extra for drizzling	2 tbsp
salt and black pepper	
ciabatta	4 slices

Chop the tomatoes and basil and mix with the garlic, vinegar, oil and salt and pepper. Cover and let infuse at room temperature for 20 minutes. Drizzle oil over the bread and toast in a griddle pan. Spoon on the tomato mixture and drizzle a little more oil over the top to serve.

Equipment

Griddle pan

Pamboli

Mallorca's famous snack, pamboli, is available at almost every café, truck stop and kiosk throughout Spain.

Serves: 1 slice per person

ripe, juicy tomatoes, at room temperature	2–3
good-quality white or brown bread	1 slice per person
garlic clove, halved	1
extra virgin olive oil (the finest you can buy)	1 tbsp
salt and black pepper	

Squish the tomatoes by hand and set aside. Toast the slices of bread on a baking tray in a 200°C (400°F/Gas 6) oven until firm, rub the garlic clove on both sides, then add a thin layer of tomato pulp.

Season well with salt and pepper and finish with a drizzle of olive oil.

Equipment

Baking pan

Roasted Grapes, Goat's Cheese, Walnuts & Thyme

Roasting grapes turns them into giant and juicy super-plump raisins, their sweetness cutting through the salty goat's cheese on this proper messy, delicious snack.

Serves: 6

seedless red grapes	20+ or a bunch
extra virgin olive oil	
walnut halves	8
soft goat's cheese	50 g (2 oz)
slices of sourdough bread, toasted	5
thyme	a bunch
salt and black pepper	

Roast the grapes in a 200°C (400°F/Gas 6) oven with a drizzle of oil and salt for 5–10 minutes until they start to split open. Remove and allow to cool.

Dry fry the walnuts in a non-stick frying pan until toasted.

Assemble dollops of cheese onto each toast, five or so grapes, walnuts and a fresh thyme leaves. Drizzle over a little juice from the roasting tin for extra sticky-sweetness. Add a pinch of pepper to finish.

Equipment

Roasting pan, non-stick frying pan

Sizzlers

Tomato, Gruyère & Dijon Filos

Cheesy, crispy, tomatoey tarts with a sharp Dijon mustard tang. Try not to eat each in one mouthful.

Serves: 6

butter, melted	75 g (2½ oz/generous ¼ cup)
filo pastry	12 sheets
Dijon mustard	1 heaped tbsp
tin chopped tomatoes	400 g (14 oz)
basil leaves	a small bunch
Gruyère cheese, grated	75 g (2½ oz)
salt and black pepper	

Using a pastry brush, lightly grease a 12-cup muffin pan. Create pastry cases by cutting the sheets of filo into squares and pressing a single square into each cup before brushing with melted butter and laying another square at a jaunty angle over the top. Repeat 2–3 more times.

Add a little mustard to each case, then add a spoon of tomato, a basil leaf and season with salt and pepper. Top with Gruyère and bake in a in a 200°C (400°F/Gas 6) oven for 15–20 minutes until golden. Serve warm.

Equipment

Pastry brush, 12-cup muffin pan

Chipotle Devils

A reworking of the classic cocktail snack Devils on Horseback, but with added devilishness.

Serves: 5

smoked streaky bacon	5–8 slices
chipotle paste	2 tsp
semi-dried prunes or dates, pitted	10
demerara sugar	2 tsp

Cut the bacon into long strips, smear on a little chipotle paste and wrap around the fruit, spearing with a cocktail stick to hold in place. Lay out on a baking tray, sprinkle with sugar and bake in a in a 200°C (400°F/Gas 6) oven for 15–20 minutes until crispy.

Equipment

Baking sheet, cocktail sticks (toothpicks)

Mini Merguez Sausage Rolls

If you fancy your sausage rolls a little spicy, add in merguez, the Middle Eastern sausage with harissa, spices and other mystery elements. It's like a souped-up, salty chorizo.

Serves: 6

puff pastry	1 sheet
egg, beaten	1
mini merguez sausages	12
fennel seeds	1 tbsp
Parmesan, finely grated	40 g (1½ oz)

Roll out the pastry, brush with beaten egg, and lay out the spicy merguez sausages in the centre of the sheet (with each sausage at a diagonal so they overlap).

Sprinkle over the fennel seeds and Parmesan, fold over the pastry and press down the edge with a fork and cut into sausage rolls. Place on a baking tray, brush with beaten egg and bake in a 180°C (356°F/Gas 4) oven for 20 minutes until raised, golden and sizzling.

Equipment
Rolling pin, baking sheet

Emmental Biscuits

These refined little crunchy, savoury biscuits are packed with cheese. What's not to love?

Serves: 8

plain (all-purpose) flour	75 g (2½ oz/½ cup)
cayenne pepper	1 tsp
cold unsalted butter, cubed, plus extra for greasing	75 g (2½oz/generous ¼ cup)
Emmental cheese, grated	75 g (2½ oz)
salt	

Sift the flour, cayenne pepper and a large pinch of salt into a food processor. Add the butter and blitz until the mixture resembles breadcrumbs. Add the cheese, then bring the mixture together with your hands. Wrap in cling film (plastic wrap) and chill for 30 minutes.

Preheat the oven to 200°C (400°F/Gas 6) and roll out the dough to a 5 mm (¼ in) thickness. Using a 5 cm (2 in) biscuit cutter, cut out rounds and space them out over two baking sheets lined with baking parchment (leave plenty of room for spreading).

Bake for 10 minutes or so or until slightly brown. Leave to cool a little, but serve warm.

Equipment
Sieve, food processor, rolling pin, 5 cm (2 in) biscuit (cookie) cutter, baking sheets

THE BEST PLACES
TO DRINK GIN

The Canary Bar,
Bath, UK

The blood red Canary Gin bar in Bath, UK, is a bit of a show off. 230 different types of gin? This little bolthole by the owners of Jane Austen-inspired Bath Gin is hidden down a simple cobbled street. Be sure to visit the delightful upstairs martini bar, if your legs can carry you.

thebathgincompany.co.uk

East London Liquor Company,
London, UK

In deepest, darkest East London, on the site of an old glue factory, is this sprawling industrial bar and work premises of the infamous ELLC. If you listen carefully (and are tipsy enough) you might just hear the old horses of yesteryear clip-clopping to their demise.

eastlondonliquorcompany.com

American Bar at The Savoy,
London, UK

In the 1930s, Harry Craddock, the Savoy's Head Bartender, created a slew of classic cocktails – and had something of a gin preoccupation. Where better to sip a few traditional classics than the bar in which they were created? Oh, and the American was award World's Best Bar in 2017.

fairmont.com/savoy

The Last Word Saloon,
Edinburgh, Scotland

Charming (read: dark, topsy turvy) little underground dive bar that makes probably the best Dirty Martini in town. A candlelit hideaway from Edinburgh's famous rainy summers.

lastwordsaloon.com

Le Glass,
Paris, France

In a city of magical, glittering bars and restaurants, Le Glass is something rather unique. For one thing, it's unerringly friendly and, another, it serves delicious drinks. Try the TU M'EXCITES! gin cocktail with its chamomile edge. Also, the chili popcorn is gratis. Merci, Le Glass!

glassparis.com

Little Branch,
NYC, USA

One of the original wave of prohibition-themed bars that sprung up in NYC in the 2000s – this tiny, dark, little basement bar has an impressive way with gin. The crowd are talky but chilled and the drinks are delicious. Impossible to find (seriously), but good luck.

@littlebranchbarny

Bemelmans Bar,
NYC, USA

Named after Ludwig Bemelmans, the author and illustrator behind the classic Madeline book series, whose artworks adorn the walls. At the iconic Carlyle Hotel, Bemelmans is the ultimate NYC cocktail bar with an impressive history: Cary Grant, Humphrey Bogart and JFK are among its former drinkers, and it appeared in the *Sex and the City* movie (but don't let that put you off).

rosewoodhotels.com

Golden Age,
Sydney, Australia

Sydney's Golden Age, the city's most celebrated and perfectly programmed arthouse cinema, has a lush, velvety, David Lynchian bar interior and a delicious drinks list – for movie-goers or mere lushes – all are welcome. A little goldmine.

ourgoldenage.com.au

Black Pearl
Melbourne, Australia

Billing itself as a neighbourhood bar in the depths of the city, Black Pearl is a hazy, late-night drinking joint that doesn't take itself too seriously. Its drinks list is impressive, and its couches squishy. Oh, and it serves sausage rolls. It won best bar in Australasia in 2017. Quite right, too.

Blackpearlbar.co.au

Museo Chicote,
Madrid, Spain

Opened in 1931, this art deco bar is Spain's oldest cocktail haunt (with an impressive list of one time guests, from Frank Sinatra to Ava Gardner). On Gran Via, Museo Chicote is often at the heart of the capital's wildest, weirdest nights out (it also appears in Almodovar's *Broken Embraces* (2009)).

grupomercadodelareina.com/
es/museo-chicote

Macera,
Madrid, Spain

In deepest, darkest, campest Chueca, cocktail bar Macera makes its own spirits using handpicked, natural ingredients, so it follows that it makes one of Madrid's most delicious G & Ts. Macera gin is infused with berries, apple, citrus, cinnamon and liquorice.

maceradrinks.com

INDEX

1724: 38
58 Gin 19

A

absinthe
  Corpse Reviver No. 2 194
  The Green Vesper 113
  Monkey Gland 81
  Tuxedo 95
Alaskan Thunder 127
almond milk: Pine Forest 118
amaretto almond liqueur:
  Totally Nuts! 198
Angel's Delight 169
Angostura bitters
  Cherry Thyme Sour 142
  Green Dragon 109
  Honey Bear Gin Punch 185
  Martinez 90
  New Fashioned 129
  Pink Gin 68
  The Queen Mum 122
  Singapore Sling 71
Aperol
  Aperol Gin Punch 186
  Gin Sour 136
  Pink Gin Spritz 156
Apocalypse Salsa 207
apple juice
  British Summer Time
  (BST) Cooler 110
  Gin Power Shot 172
Arizona Cooler 123
Artichoke Dip 205
aubergines: Baba Ganoush 206
Aviation 76

B

Baba Ganoush 206
bacon
  Chipotle Devils 210
  The Ultimate Hangover
  Bacon Roll 201
bananas: Totally Nuts! 198
Bath Gin 28
Bathtub Gin 22
Bay Leaf & Green Tea Martini 104
Bay Leaf Gin 55
Beach House 115
Beefeater 24: 24
beer: Honey Beer Punch 184
Bees Knees 159
Bénédictine: Singapore Sling 71
Bergamot Tea Martini 101
biscuits: Emmental Biscuits 211
blackberries
  Blackberry & Lavender Spritz 186
  Bramble 72

Blood Orange Gin & Tonic 177
Bloody Sour Mix 62
Bloom 26
blueberries: Summer Blueberry
  Cocktail 188
Borage Citrus Fizz 150
Borage Syrup 59
Boston Tea Party 85
The Botanist Islay Dry Gin 33
Bradley's Kina Tonic 38
Bramble 72
Breakfast Martini 174
brines 63
British Summer Time (BST)
  Cooler 110
Bronx 84
Bruschetta 208
Butler's Lemongrass & Cardamom 21

C

Camembert: Hot Camembert &
  Salsa Verde 205
Campari
  Negroni 82
  Pink Gin Spritz 156
  Sloe Gin & Tempranillo Negroni 125
Caorunn 27
Chambord: French Martini 99
Champagne
  French 77: 153
  Royal Orange Blossom 168
  The Rudolph 126
  Southside Royale 158
Chartreuse: Alaskan Thunder 127
Cheddar: Dirty Toasted Cheese 208
cherries
  Cherry & Thyme Syrup 60
  Cherry French 75: 137
  Cherry Thyme Sour 142
  Sour Cherry Sling 151
cherry brandy: Singapore Sling 71
Cherry Heering liqueur:
  Cherry French 75: 137
Chipotle Devils 210
Classic Gin Martini 88
Classic Sour Mix 62
Clover Club 80
cocktail tricks 50–1
coconut water
  Beach House 115
  Coconut G & T 114
coffee: Turbo G & T 198
Cointreau
  Angel's Delight 169
  Corpse Reviver No. 2 194
  Singapore Sling 71
  Sour Cherry Sling 151
  White Lady 119
The Colby 128
Collagin 24

Conker Spirit 22
Cornflower Martini 97
Cornflower Syrup 59
Corpse Reviver No. 2 194
cranberry juice
  Arizona Cooler 123
  The Colby 128
  Long Beach Ice Tea 131
  The Snoop 182
crème de cassis: Blackberry &
  Lavender Spritz 186
crème de menthe: Green Dragon 109
crème de mûre: Bramble 72
crème de violette
  Aviation 76
  Violet Fizz 153
cucumber
  Cucumber Lemonade 176
  Cucumber Mint Gin Fizz 141
  Cucumber Rose Fizz 145
  Smashed Cucumber 117

D

dips 205–7
Dirty Martini 88
Dirty Toasted Cheese 208
Dubonnet: The Queen Mum 122

E

Earl Grey Tea: Bergamot
  Tea Martini 101
East London Liquor Company
  London Dry 31
elderflower cordial
  British Summer Time (BST)
  Cooler 110
  Gooseberry Gin Fizz 147
elderflower liqueur
  French 77: 153
  Red Wine Gin Sour 134
Elderflower Martini 97
elderflower syrup: Marmajito 196
elderflower tonic water:
  Watermelon G & T 178
Emmental Biscuits 211
equipment 42–5

F

Fentimans 35
Fever-Tree 35
Few American Gin 27
Floradora 75
Four Pillars 19
Frangelico Hazelnut Liqueur: Totally
  Nuts! 198
French 75 Punch 189

French 77: 153
French Martini 99
Frozen G & T 182

G

G & T Pancakes with Lemon Syrup .. 200
Galliano: Aperol Gin Punch 186
The Gibson 94
Gilbert Grape 148
Gimlet 92
gin 9–12
Gin & Jam Cocktail 171
Gin Mare 26
Gin Power Shot 172
Gin St Clements 174
ginger ale
　Floradora 75
　Gin Buck 77
ginger beer: Sloe Ginger 162
Ginger Gin 55
Ginger Greyhound 166
ginger juice: Gin Power Shot 172
ginger: Rhubarb, Ginger & Star Anise
　Syrup 58
glasses 48–9
goat's cheese: Roasted Grapes, Goat's
　Cheese, Walnuts & Thyme 209
Goldy 25
Gooseberry Gin Fizz 147
Grand Marnier
　Boston Tea Party 85
　Breakfast Martini 174
grapefruit juice
　Aperol Gin Punch 186
　Arizona Cooler 123
　Bloody Sour Mix 62
　Ginger Greyhound 166
　Grapefruit & Tarragon Collins 120
　Lillet Rose 173
　Pink Gin Spritz 156
　Salty Dog 74
grapefruit soda: Rosemary Gin
　Paloma 163
grapes
　Gilbert Grape 148
　Roasted Grapes, Goat's Cheese,
　　Walnuts & Thyme 209
Green Dragon 109
Green Snapper 165
The Green Vesper 113
grenadine
　Angel's Delight 169
　Monkey Gland 81
　Singapore Sling 71
Gruyère: Tomato, Gruyère & Dijon
　Filos 210

H

Halloumi, Harrisa & Naan Bread .. 204
Hayman's 1850 Reserve 25
Hendrick's 29
Highwayman Gin 31
honey
　Bees Knees 159
　Honey Bear Gin Punch 185
　Honey Beer Punch 184
horseradish
　Red Snapper 164
　Smoked Mackerel & Horseradish .. 206
Hot Gin Punch 190

I

ice cream: Totally Nuts! 198
Indi & Co. 37
infusions 54–5

J

Jinzu 28

K

Kahlúa Coffee Liqueur:
　Turbo G & T 198

L

Lavender & Rose Syrup 57
Lavender Gin 55
Lavender Martini 103
lemon juice
　Aviation 76
　Bay Leaf & Green Tea Martini 104
　Bees Knees 159
　Borage Citrus Fizz 150
　Bramble 72
　Breakfast Martini 174
　Cherry French 75: 137
　Classic Sour Mix 62
　Clover Club 80
　The Colby 128
　Cornflower Martini 97
　Corpse Reviver No. 2 194
　Cucumber Lemonade 176
　Cucumber Mint Gin Fizz 141
　Cucumber Rose Fizz 145
　Elderflower Martini 97
　Floradora 75
　French 75 Punch 189
　French 77: 153
　G & T Pancakes with
　　Lemon Syrup 200
　Gin & Jam Cocktail 171
　Gin Buck 77
　Gin Sour 136

Gin St Clements 174
Honey Beer Punch 184
Hot Gin Punch 190
Lillet Rose 173
Long Island Iced Tea 78
New Orleans Fizz 146
Red Snapper 164
Red Wine Gin Sour 134
Rhubarb Collins 152
Rhubarb Sour 138
Silver Fizz 197
Simple Sour Mix 62
Sloe Gin Cooler 125
Spiced Rhubarb & Rose Ramos
　Gin Fizz 144
Tom Collins 70
Violet Fizz 153
Watermelon G & T 178
White Lady 119
Lemon Verbena Cooler 112
lemonade
　Gooseberry Gin Fizz 147
　Naked Peach 160
Lillet Rose Vermouth
　Lillet Rose 173
　The Vesper 91
lime juice
　Aperol Gin Punch 186
　Beach House 115
　Blackberry & Lavender Spritz 186
　Blood Orange Gin & Tonic 177
　Cherry Thyme Sour 142
　Classic Sour Mix 62
　Frozen G & T 182
　Gilbert Grape 148
　Gimlet 92
　Gin Power Shot 172
　Gin Rickey 140
　Gooseberry Gin Fizz 147
　Green Dragon 109
　Green Snapper 165
　Naked Peach 160
　New Orleans Fizz 146
　Perfect G & T 68
　Simple Sour Mix 62
　Singapore Sling 71
　Smashed Cucumber 117
　The Snoop 182
　Sour Cherry Sling 151
　The Southside 82
　Spiced Rhubarb & Rose Ramos
　　Gin Fizz 144
　Summer Blueberry Cocktail 188
limes
　Coconut G & T 114
　Lemon Verbena Cooler 112
　Naked Peach 160
　Southside Royale 158
　Long Beach Ice Tea 131
Long Island Iced Tea 78
Lychee Martini 102

M

mackerel: Smoked Mackerel & Horseradish 206
Madeira wine: Hot Gin Punch 190
mandarin vodka: Royal Orange Blossom 168
maraschino liqueur
  Aviation 76
  Martinez 90
  Saketini 108
  Tuxedo 95
Marmajito 196
marmalade
  Breakfast Martini 174
  Marmajito 196
Martin Miller's 20
Martinez 90
The Melbourne Gin Company 27
Merchant's Heart 36
Mini Merguez Sausage Rolls 211
Monkey 47: 23
Monkey Gland 81
Moonshine Kid's Dog's Nose 20

N

naan bread: Halloumi, Harrisa & Naan Bread 204
Naked Peach 160
Negroni 82
New Fashioned 129
New Orleans Fizz 146
New York Distilling Company Dorothy Parker 30
Nice Pear 131
No. 209: 21
nuts: Totally Nuts! 198

O

olive brine: Dirty Martini 88
The One Gin 29
orange bitters
  Alaskan Thunder 127
  Aperol Gin Punch 186
  Bees Knees 159
  Bergamot Tea Martini 101
  Borage Citrus Fizz 150
  The Colby 128
  French 75 Punch 189
  French 77: 153
  Gin Sour 136
  Lavender Martini 103
  Lillet Rose 173
  New Fashioned 129
  New Orleans Fizz 146
  Park Avenue Martini 98
  Perfect G & T 68
  Red Wine Gin Sour 134
  Rhubarb Collins 152

Silver Fizz 197
Tuxedo 95
orange blossom water: The Queen Mum 122
orange juice
  Blood Orange Gin & Tonic 177
  Bloody Sour Mix 62
  Bronx 84
  Gin St Clements 174
  Hot Gin Punch 190
  Monkey Gland 81
  Royal Orange Blossom 168
  The Snoop 182
orange liqueur: Long Island Iced Tea 78
Owen's Craft Mixers 39

P

Pamboli 209
pancakes: G & T Pancakes with Lemon Syrup 200
Park Avenue Martini 98
peaches: Naked Peach 160
pear juice: Nice Pear 131
Perfect G & T 68
Pine Forest 118
Pine Tip Syrup 60
pineapple
  Apocalypse Salsa 207
  Cheese & Pineapple 204
  Hot Gin Punch 190
pineapple juice
  French Martini 99
  Green Snapper 165
  Park Avenue Martini 98
  Singapore Sling 71
  The Snoop 182
Pink Gin 68
Pink Gin Spritz 156
pomegranate juice: Sloe Ginger 162
Prosecco
  Aperol Gin Punch 186
  Blackberry & Lavender Spritz 186
  Cherry French 75: 137
  French 75 Punch 189
  Honey Bear Gin Punch 185
prunes: Chipotle Devils 210

Q

The Queen Mum 122

R

raspberry jam: Gin & Jam Cocktail 171
raspberry purée: Clover Club 80
Red Snapper 164

Red Wine Gin Sour 134
reductions: tempranillo reduction 57
rhubarb bitters: Salty Dog 74
Rhubarb Collins 152
Rhubarb Gin 54
Rhubarb, Ginger & Star Anise Syrup 58
Rhubarb Sour 138
Roasted Grapes, Goat's Cheese, Walnuts & Thyme 209
rose petals: Lavender & Rose Syrup 57
rosemary bitters:
  Rosemary Gin Paloma 163
  Rosemary Gin Paloma 163
  Rosemary Syrup 61
rosewater
  Cherry French 75: 137
  Spiced Rhubarb & Rose Ramos Gin Fizz 144
Royal Orange Blossom 168
The Rudolph 126
rum
  Boston Tea Party 85
  Long Beach Ice Tea 131
  Long Island Iced Tea 78

S

Saketini 108
Salcombe Gin Start Point 23
salsa
  Apocalypse Salsa 207
  Hot Camembert & Salsa Verde 205
Salty Dog 74
sausage rolls: Mini Merguez Sausage Rolls 211
Schweppes 36
Silver Fizz 197
Simple Sour Mix 62
Singapore Sling 71
Sloe & Star Anise Gin 54
Sloe Gin 54
Sloe Gin & Tempranillo Negroni 125
Sloe Gin Cooler 125
Sloe Ginger 162
Smashed Cucumber 117
The Snoop 182
soda water
  Borage Citrus Fizz 150
  British Summer Time (BST) Cooler 110
  Cucumber Lemonade 176
  Gilbert Grape 148
  Gin Rickey 140
  Lemon Verbena Cooler 112
  New Orleans Fizz 146
  Rhubarb Collins 152
  Silver Fizz 197
  Sloe Gin Cooler 125

Smashed Cucumber 117
Sour Cherry Sling 151
Spiced Rhubarb & Rose Ramos
    Gin Fizz 144
Tom Collins 70
Violet Fizz 153
Sour Cherry Sling 151
sours 62
The Southside 82
Southside Royale 158
spices: Hot Gin Punch 190
Square Root 37
St. George Terroir Gin 32
St-Germain
    The Colby 128
    Elderflower Martini 97
    The Rudolph 126
star anise: Rhubarb, Ginger & Star
    Anise Syrup 58
Strangelove 39
Summer Blueberry Cocktail 188
syrups
    Cherry & Thyme Syrup 60
    Cornflower Or Borage Syrup 59
    flavoured syrups 61
    Lavender & Rose Syrup 57
    Pine Tip Syrup 60
    Rhubarb, Ginger & Star
        Anise Syrup 58
    Simple Syrup 58
    Spiced Brown Sugar Syrup 59

T
Tanqueray No. Ten 30
Tempranillo Reduction 57
tequila: Long Island Iced Tea 78
Tia Maria: Boston Tea Party 85
Tom Collins 70
tomato juice: Red Snapper 164
tomatoes
    Bruschetta 208
    Pamboli 209
    Tomato, Gruyère & Dijon Filos 210
tonic syrup: Frozen G & T 182
tonic water **35–9**
    Blood Orange Gin & Tonic 177
    Coconut G & T 114
    Cucumber Mint Gin Fizz 141
    G & T Pancakes with
        Lemon Syrup 200
    Gin St Clements 174
    Grapefruit & Tarragon Collins 120
    Marmajito 196
    Perfect G & T 68
    Turbo G & T 198
Top Note Tonics 39
Totally Nuts! 198

triple sec
    Cherry Thyme Sour 142
    Long Beach Ice Tea 131
    Park Avenue Martini 98
    Rhubarb Sour 138
Turbo G & T 198
Tuxedo 95

V
vermouth
    Bronx 84
    Classic Gin Martini 88
    Cornflower Martini 97
    Corpse Reviver No. 2 194
    Dirty Martini 88
    The Gibson 94
    Lavender Martini 103
    Lychee Martini 102
    Martinez 90
    Negroni 82
    Park Avenue Martini 98
    Tuxedo 95
The Vesper 91
Violet Fizz 153
vodka
    Bay Leaf & Green Tea Martini 104
    Bergamot Tea Martini 101
    Boston Tea Party 85
    Elderflower Martini 97
    The Green Vesper 113
    Long Beach Ice Tea 131
    Long Island Iced Tea 78
    Summer Blueberry Cocktail 188
    The Vesper 91

W
Watermelon G & T 178
White Lady 119
Williams Chase 33
wine: Red Wine Gin Sour 134
Worcestershire sauce:
    Red Snapper 164

ABOUT
THE
AUTHOR

Dan Jones is a writer living in London. Formerly the Shopping Editor at *i-D* magazine, and *Time Out's* Style editor, he considers himself one of the world's foremost cocktail enjoyers. He is the author of *The Mixer's Manual; Man Made; The Gentleman's Guide to Grooming; 50 Queers Who Changed The World; Gin: Shake, Muddle, Stir; Rum: Shake, Muddle, Stir* and *Tequila: Shake, Muddle, Stir*. His favourite gin cocktail is an extremely Dirty Martini.

ACKNOWLEDGEMENTS

Thanks to superstar illustrator and designer Evi O., and the dream team of Jacqui Melville, Kathy Kordalis, Wei Tang and Radar at Ginger Whisk, Kentaro Poteliakhoff at Rooms of Clapton, plus Senior Editor Molly Ahuja, and all at Hardie Grant.

Published in 2018 by Hardie Grant Books,
an imprint of Hardie Grant Publishing

Hardie Grant Books (London)
5th & 6th Floors
52–54 Southwark Street
London SE1 1UN

Hardie Grant Books (Melbourne)
Building 1, 658 Church Street
Richmond, Victoria 3121

hardiegrantbooks.com

British Library Cataloguing-in-Publication Data. A catalogue
record for this book is available from the British Library.

The Big Book of Gin by Dan Jones

ISBN: 978-1-78488-193-1

Publisher: Kate Pollard
Senior Editor: Molly Ahuja
Publishing Assistant: Eila Purvis
Additional Recipe Development: Seb Munsch
Art Direction: Evi O. Studio | Evi O
Illustrators: Evi O. Studio | Evi O & Susan Le
Photographer: Jacqui Melville
Food styling: Kathy Kordalis
Prop styling: Wei Tang
Editor: Kay Delves
Proofreader: Wendy Hobson
Indexer: Cathy Heath

Colour Reproduction by p2d
Printed and bound in China by Leo Paper Group